The Heart of Faith

Following Christ in the Church of England

Edited by
Andrew Atherstone

Lutterworth Press

The Lutterworth Press
P.O. Box 60
Cambridge
CB1 2NT
United Kingdom

www.lutterworth.com
publishing@lutterworth.com

ISBN: 978 0 7188 3072 4

British Library Cataloguing in Publication Data
A record is available from the British Library

Dedication

For Barbara Atherstone, on her ninetieth birthday,
and in memory of Walter Atherstone (1912-1995),
lifelong Anglicans and faithful followers of Christ

Contents

Contributors

Andrew Atherstone is tutor in history and doctrine, and Latimer research fellow, at Wycliffe Hall, Oxford. He is author of *Oxford's Protestant Spy* (2007), *The Martyrs of Mary Tudor* (second edition, 2007) and *Oxford* (2008).

Nigel Atkinson is vicar of Knutsford in Cheshire. He is author of *Richard Hooker and the Authority of Scripture, Tradition and Reason* (second edition, 2005).

David Bebbington is professor of history at the University of Stirling. His books include *Evangelicalism in Modern Britain* (1989), *Victorian Nonconformity* (1992), *The Mind of Gladstone* (2004) and *The Dominance of Evangelicalism* (2005).

Roger Beckwith was librarian and warden of Latimer House, Oxford for more than thirty years. His books include *The Old Testament Canon of the New Testament Church* (1985), *Calendar and Chronology, Jewish and Christian* (1996) and *Elders in Every City* (2004).

Gerald Bray is director of research for the Latimer Trust and research professor at Beeson Divinity School in Birmingham, Alabama. His books include *The Doctrine of God* (1993), *Biblical Interpretation* (1996), *Creeds, Councils and Christ* (second edition, 1997), *Documents of the English Reformation* (second edition, 2004) and *Yours is the Kingdom* (2007).

John Coffey is professor of early modern history at the University of Leicester. His books include *Politics, Religion and the British Revolutions* (1997), *Persecution and Toleration in Protestant England* (2000) and *John Goodwin and the Puritan Revolution* (2006).

Graham Cray is bishop of Maidstone, in Canterbury Diocese, and was previously principal of Ridley Hall, Cambridge. His books include *Disciples and Citizens* (2007) and (as co-author) *Making Sense of Generation Y* (2006) and *Mission-Shaped Youth* (2007).

Mark Dever is senior pastor of Capitol Hill Baptist Church, Washington DC. His books include *Richard Sibbes* (2000), *Nine Marks of a Healthy Church* (second edition, 2004), *The Message of the New Testament* (2005) and *The Message of the Old Testament* (2006).

Alan Munden is assistant minister at Jesmond Parish Church, Newcastle upon Tyne. His books include *A Cheltenham Gamaliel: Dean Close of Cheltenham* (1997), *A History of St Luke's Church, Cheltenham* (2004) and *A Light in a Dark Place: Jesmond Parish Church* (2006).

Michael Nazir-Ali is bishop of Rochester and was previously general-secretary of the Church Mission Society. His books include *Mission and Dialogue* (1998), *Citizens and Exiles* (1998), *Shapes of the Church to Come* (2001), *Conviction and Conflict* (2006) and *The Unique and Universal Christ* (2008)

Mark Smith is university lecturer in English local and social history at the University of Oxford. His books include *Religion in Industrial Society* (1994) and (as editor) *Evangelicalism in the Church of England* (2004) and *British Evangelical Identities* (2008).

Michael Ward is an Anglican minister and was chaplain of Peterhouse, Cambridge 2004-2007. He is author of *Planet Narnia: The Seven Heavens in the Imagination of C.S. Lewis* (2008) and co-editor of *Heresies and How to Avoid Them* (2007).

Martin Wellings is a Methodist minister in the Oxford Circuit and president of the World Methodist Historical Society. His publications include *Evangelicals Embattled* (2003) and *Evangelicals in Methodism* (2005).

David Wells is the Andrew Mutch distinguished professor of historical and systematic theology at Gordon-Conwell Theological Seminary in Massachusetts. His books include *No Place for Truth* (1993), *God in the Wasteland* (1994), *Losing our Virtue* (1998) and *Above all Earthly Pow'rs* (2005).

John Wolffe is professor of religious history at the Open University. His books include *The Protestant Crusade in Great Britain* (1991), *God and Greater Britain* (1994), *Great Deaths* (2000) and *The Expansion of Evangelicalism* (2006).

Acknowledgements

This book originally began as an idea at the Theological Work Group of the Latimer Trust and thanks are due to the Trust for offering a generous grant towards its publication. I am also grateful to the excellent team of authors for contributing so cheerfully in the midst of their many pressing academic, administrative and pastoral responsibilities. Although the subjects of this book were all members of the Church of England, the writers are scholars and ministers both interdenominational (Anglican, Baptist, Congregationalist, Methodist) and international.

Andrew Atherstone
April, 2008

Introduction

Andrew Atherstone

This short book aims to appeal to anyone with an interest in Anglican history and identity. It does not examine institutions, or structures, or the rapidly changing winds of ecclesiastical politics. Instead it explores the teaching of sixteen individuals – significant men and women who have been part of the Anglican movement, spread over many centuries. These vignettes are not mini-biographies and do not focus upon their careers (which can be found in the *Oxford Dictionary of National Biography* and many history textbooks), but rather ask questions about their theological passions and convictions. How did they understand their relationship with God, the incarnation and atonement of Christ, the role of the Holy Spirit, the authority of the Bible and the mission of the church? What was driving them? What did they teach? What was their vision for God's people? How did they work out their Christian discipleship in practice? In short, this book aims to get to 'the heart of faith' of these famous Anglicans.

Of course, a volume which is dominated by 'dead white men' cannot claim to be representative of worldwide Anglicanism, which is a vibrant international phenomenon. The focus of this book is limited to the Church of England, which is but one small part of this diverse movement. The centre of influence in the Anglican world has shifted in the last generation from Britain and North America to the Global South, where dynamic evangelism and exponential church growth are most often seen. It is no longer Canterbury which calls the tune. Nevertheless the history and roots of the Church of England go back much further and much deeper than most other Anglican provinces. The 'Anglican Communion' is a new concept and the earliest known use of the phrase dates from only 1847. 'Anglican-*ism*' was also coined in the early nineteenth century. But *Ecclesia Anglicana* (the church of the English) has been in existence for a millennium and a half, since the Roman and Celtic missions under Augustine and Columba respectively, which established Christianity on

British shores in the early middle ages.

The sixteen men and women examined in these chapters lived and worked, preached and wrote, over the many generations since that time – from the late seventh century to the early twenty-first. They witnessed the widest range of political, cultural and ecclesial developments and traumas, from Viking Invasion to Peasants' Revolt, Renaissance to Reformation, Civil War to Enlightenment, and beyond. The English worlds which they inhabited were in many ways unrecognisably different. Their life situations were also diverse – from the celibate monk to the married mother of eighteen children; from the innovative scientist to the captivating poet; from the urbane scholar to the popular preacher to the tenacious politician. Yet they held in common their loyal membership of the Church of England.

What of their theological diversity? This book does not claim to reflect the full range of opinions held within the Church of England, in all their colourful confusion. Evangelicals predominate, though by no means all can be categorised in that way. Think for example, of the Venerable Bede, Archbishop John Peckham, Richard Hooker, Robert Boyle, Susanna Wesley or C.S. Lewis, who came from different streams of Anglican thinking. Furthermore, those evangelical Anglicans who do make an appearance were far from homogenous – contrast, for example, the divergent attitudes of J.C. Ryle and Frances Ridley Havergal to the holiness movement of the nineteenth century; or the disparate approaches to the charismatic movement and the gifts of the Holy Spirit, as represented by John Stott and David Watson. Nevertheless, for all their theological diversity and distinctives, the men and women introduced in these pages showed by their lives and teaching a clear commitment to a generous Christian orthodoxy. They disagreed, sometimes sharply, on many secondary issues, but they held the Christian essentials in common. They force us to think afresh about what it means to be a member of the Church of England, and about what lies at the heart of Anglican identity.

Before the Reformation

Gerald Bray

How far back in time does Anglicanism extend? The idea that Anglicanism is a distinct branch of Christianity comparable to Rome and the Eastern churches first gained currency in the nineteenth century, but the Tractarians who promoted it believed that it could be traced back to the Anglo-Saxon and Celtic churches of the early middle ages. Antiquarians before them had gone back to the legendary origins of Christianity in Britain, but by the nineteenth century only eccentrics continued to believe that Joseph of Arimathea had brought the faith to Glastonbury in apostolic times.

The Tractarians set little store by these ancient legends and confined themselves to historically verifiable sources, but this still took them back to St Augustine of Canterbury and the mission which he established in Kent on 26 May 597. The Church of Ireland did not hesitate to trace its own roots to Patrick himself and the fact that the ancient Celtic church was not in communion with Rome until the eighth century only added to its appeal. At the other extreme were those who maintained that the origins of Anglicanism could not be dated further back than the sixteenth-century reformation. Roman Catholics naturally insisted on this, but so did many Protestants, albeit for totally different reasons. To them the medieval Church of England was both corrupt and subservient to Rome, and Henry VIII's revolt was a great liberation, not only of the English people but of the Christian gospel itself. In their eyes, John Wycliffe (c. 1330-1384) was the 'morning star' of the reformation, whose great work of Bible translation came to brilliant fruition in the New Testament of William Tyndale (1525). That in turn led to the foundational texts of classical Anglicanism, the Authorized Version of 1611 and the various recensions of the *Book of Common Prayer* (1549-1662). Some Protestant nonconformists went even further and said that Anglicanism as we understand it did not emerge until the dissenters finally hived off from the Church of England, leaving only a conforming episcopal remnant to claim the name of Anglican.

Today, these different opinions have largely given way to what may aptly be called a *de facto* consensus. Most students of the subject now agree that Anglicanism can be traced back to the sixteenth-century reformation, albeit in a somewhat embryonic form, and that it developed a distinctive ecclesiological position in the struggle against puritanism. Begun by Richard Hooker and John Whitgift in the late sixteenth century and continued by various high church divines into the early 1700s, the defining moment of this struggle was the great ejection (1662), a fact to which the continuing use of the 1662 Prayer Book bears witness. It was in this form that Anglicanism was exported and became a worldwide communion, and it is to those who have been shaped within that framework that the name 'Anglican' is most naturally applied today.

Where does this leave the pre-reformation Church of England? What about the Celtic churches, which played such an important part in the evangelization of England, as well as of the other countries of the British Isles? On the one hand, leaving aside the temporary and essentially accidental breach of communion with Rome, it is now generally agreed that they were an integral part of the undivided Western church until the early sixteenth century. Anselm of Canterbury (c. 1033-1109) may have been primate of all England but he could hardly be called an Anglican, and to describe St David or St Columba in that way would be incongruous, not to say absurd. On the other hand, the post-reformation churches of England (including Wales) and Ireland inherited the buildings, structures and personnel of the pre-reformation church and did remarkably little to alter them. The monasteries were dissolved, it is true, but much of their heritage was reclaimed by parish churches, schools and the universities, and the ecclesiastical law remained essentially unchanged. A man training for ordination in 1600 had to work harder and study different theological ideas than his predecessors of a century before, but his career pathway in the church was pretty much the same as theirs had been. He would have gone to the same universities, applied for the same ordination in the traditional way, and found a living within a parish system which was already centuries old.

The break with Rome in 1534 did not appear as a 'Protestant reformation' at the time, and it was only in the reign of Queen Elizabeth I (1558-1603) that most people became conscious that the Church of England had become something different from medieval Catholicism – though quite what that something was, was hard to say. Those in the know recognised their debt to Martin Luther, but the English had not followed developments in Germany or Scandinavia after the great reformer's death and they did not think of themselves as Lutherans. The Swiss reformers, including both Calvin and Bullinger, were more influential, but the presbyterian church polity and civic republicanism of the Swiss cantons did not fit the English scene, and there was always the more clearly reformed Scottish kirk to remind everyone of just how far the southern kingdom still had to travel if it was ever to be truly 'reformed'. The reformed Church of England was definitely not a Lollard body either. Modern research has revealed that Lollardy survived in England into the sixteenth century, but it had no discernible impact on the English reformation and seems to have merged into it without leaving much trace. When English divines looked for a justification of their church, it was primarily to the Fathers that they turned. They did not claim to have survived the middle ages unscathed; rather, they were returning to a situation which had prevailed before the great Hildebrandine reforms of the mid-eleventh century. Conveniently for them, the introduction of these reforms into England was connected with the Norman conquest of 1066, and so the Anglo-Saxon period could be made to appear as a golden age of pure religion before the corruption of the medieval church set in. That was another historical myth, although the 550 years of Anglo-Saxon Christianity did continue to leave their mark on later centuries, and even the post-conquest *Ecclesia Anglicana* had particularities, if not peculiarities, which helped to shape the reformed Church of England. It is to these threads of particularity and continuity that we have to look for antecedents to what we now think of as Anglicanism.

Bede (c. 673-735)

No student of English history can escape the towering figure of Bede. In an intellectual and spiritual sense, it can even be said that he 'invented' the English church and nation. When Bede first took up his pen, his audience consisted of a disparate group of Germanic tribes, intermingled to a limited extent with the earlier Celtic inhabitants of Britain. But when he finally laid it down, he was speaking to an English Christian nation, ecclesiastically (though not yet politically) united and increasingly conscious of its divinely-appointed destiny. To the extent that Bede saw the English as chosen by God in a way that other nations were not, he is an authentic precursor of Anglicanism and a harbinger of that elusive distinctiveness which would characterise the post-reformation English church. Today Bede is known mainly as a historian, without whose work our knowledge of the Christianization of England would be much poorer than it is. His sense of the foreordained destiny of his people comes out very clearly in the famous story he tells of how Pope Gregory I sent a mission to them. Seeing English slaves being sold in the market at

Rome, Gregory asked where they were from. On being told they were Angles, he made his famous quip: 'Not Angles but angels'. He went on to make another pun on the place name Deira, which comes out in Latin as *de ira* ('out of wrath'), because his mission would lead the English out of God's wrath into salvation. Finally, the name of their king (Aelle) was turned by Gregory into Alleluia, the song of triumph which the Christian church would soon be singing in Aelle's land. Bede even reported that Gregory wanted to travel north himself, but was prevented from doing so because he became bishop of Rome. Instead, he had to send his friend Augustine, whose name inevitably recalled the greatest doctor of the Western church. As a historian, Bede is honest enough to inform his readers that the story of the slave market is unlikely to have been true, but he tells it for another reason, which to him was so important that it justified his lapse of scholarly judgement. He wants the English to understand that they are a chosen race, who have been rescued from damnation and charged by God with the task of spreading his gospel to the ends of the earth.

That soon became a reality, as English missionaries went to Germany and Scandinavia, doing much to win those lands for Christ. Though not an admirer of the Welsh (whom he accused of having failed to preach the gospel to the English), Bede had great respect for Irish scholarship and much of his work was dependent on it. For him, Christian England was not Anglo-Saxon so much as Anglo-Celtic, as learned monks from the north and west came to instruct his people and join forces with them for the great work of evangelization abroad. Modern sensitivities make it difficult for us to relate to this heritage nowadays, for fear of appearing to be racist, but that was not Bede's intention. To him, God's providence was an act of grace to the undeserving and the destiny of his people was a privilege they had been granted, not a right which they had deserved. Whatever we may think of it now, there is no doubt that this spirit played a major part in British overseas expansion in modern times. The British Empire was never a crudely commercial or imperialistic enterprise. It always had a redemptive aspect to it, a missionary purpose which can still be seen today in the way that the church plays a prophetic role in so many countries of the Commonwealth.

Admittedly, the same was true of other colonial empires, but neither the Spanish, the French nor the Portuguese left so distinctive a spiritual legacy behind them. Great powers that they were, they were servants of an international Catholicism which continues to claim the fruits of their missionary labours. The British however, exported their own brands of Christianity, of which Anglicanism has been the most important and distinctive part.

It is not an accident that Anglicans played a major role in the struggle against apartheid in South Africa, nor is it by chance that countries as different as Kenya and Nigeria have outspoken and influential Anglican leaders. In taking the Christian faith around the world, the Church of England took that sense of God-given purpose which so inspired Bede, and helped to create a world in which English is the common language and the values of English democracy and fair play have become universal ideals. The English themselves may not realise it, but a sense of destiny has taken Bede's church and people a very long way indeed, and the spirit he instilled in them still animates the Anglican Communion around the world.

Even if Bede had been no more than a historian, his greatness would still be assured, but he was much more than that. He was an extremely learned student of the Bible and of the church fathers, whose wisdom he distilled in his extensive commentaries, which became standard works in the middle ages. He had a comprehensive vision of the Scriptures as a theological unity and developed that insight to a degree which would not be seen again until John Calvin. His knowledge was limited by the constraints of his time, but it was nevertheless prodigious, and his judgements are often sounder than one might expect. He was no friend of allegory, and was prepared to draw on the rich resources of the Greek tradition, particularly in its Antiochene form as a supplement to his Western, Latin inheritance. Here too, Bede seems curiously proto-Anglican. A love for the Fathers has always distinguished the Anglican tradition, as has Bede's balance between the two major traditions of theological thought which we have inherited from antiquity. Where others have tended to stick to their own and develop Catholic, Orthodox, Lutheran or Reformed theological traditions, Anglicans have always felt free to range across the whole spectrum of Christian thought and take from every tradition whatever they find of value in it. This is surely one reason why Anglicanism is so hard to classify in relation to other forms of Christianity – it has never sought to be a tradition as such, but has always aimed to be 'mere Christianity', the fulness of the faith once delivered to the saints. Internally, this has given Anglicans a freedom to develop a church broad enough to find room for almost every expression of the faith, even if it has also led to internal divisions and occasional secessions by those who cannot stomach such diversity. Externally, this catholicity may also explain why, at least until recently, Anglicans could move freely among and find common ground with every other kind of Christian, from Plymouth Brethren at one end of the spectrum to Oriental Orthodox at the other.

John Peckham (c. 1230-1292)

Bede is widely known, at least by name, but few have heard of John Peckham, who was Archbishop of Canterbury from 1279 to 1292. This is not surprising, but his importance for the Church of England should not be underestimated. Before becoming archbishop, Peckham spent many years lecturing in Paris and in Rome, and he even took on the formidable Thomas Aquinas in open disputation. He defended the traditional Augustinian theology against Aquinas' Aristotelian synthesis, and to the end of his days he resisted the importation of Thomism into England. Although intellectually gifted, Peckham never fell into the trap of intellectualism and promoted spiritual revival as the best way to strengthen the church. This was especially noticeable in Wales, which was conquered by England during his time at Canterbury (1283). Peckham lost no time in trying to integrate the Welsh church into the English one, but although he might nowadays be accused of 'imperialism', his chief aim was to promote the spiritual welfare of the Welsh people, whose church had long suffered from poverty and neglect.

As archbishop, Peckham was a diligent pastor and visited all eighteen dioceses of the province of Canterbury, an almost unheard-of achievement at that time. He stood up for the rights of the church against the powerful King Edward I and in the process laid the foundations of an independent ecclesiastical jurisdiction, which survives to this day. Peckham forced the secular authorities to recognise the church's juridical autonomy (1286) and in 1291 he oversaw a comprehensive clerical tax reform which covered the whole of the British Isles and remained in force until the reformation. One of his first acts upon taking office was to legislate against 'pluralism', or the holding of more than one benefice by a single individual. Pluralism was popular with the king because it enabled him to provide an income for his own civil servants, many of whom were ordained clergy on permanent secondment to the crown, but it was harmful to the pastoral ministry. Peckham did not succeed in stamping pluralism out (that did not happen until 1838!) but his courageous stand, which defied the interests of both the king and of many of the clergy, stands out as a model for the English church – and one which unfortunately was not followed during the sixteenth-century reformation.

In 1281 Peckham held a provincial synod at Lambeth where he issued his famous decree on clerical education, known by its opening words as *Ignorantia sacerdotum* ('the ignorance of priests'). Faced with deplorably low standards of ministerial training, Peckham devised a curriculum of studies for those who desired holy orders. This curriculum consisted of the Apostles' Creed, the Ten Commandments, Jesus' summary of the law, the seven works of mercy, the seven deadly sins (and their effects), the seven cardinal virtues and the seven sacraments. Though not specifically mentioned in this canon, we may add the Lord's Prayer and the *Ave Maria* to the list, since both are found in the summary given by the Bishop of Exeter only a few years later (around 1287) and both had already figured in earlier church legislation. Priests were instructed to teach these things to their people, but it is clear that first they had to learn them themselves.

The immediate impact of this legislation is impossible to gauge, but Peckham set a standard which was still being cited at the time of the reformation and later. His main source was clearly the *Sentences* of Peter Lombard, who taught in Paris and became that city's bishop shortly before he died in 1160. But if the material was not original, his intention that it should be taught to everyone in the church, clergy and laity alike, surely was. Peckham believed that the clergy were servants of their people at a time when the temptation was to exalt them above the laity as sacrificing priests. He was fighting against the tide, but when the time eventually came to print primers and catechisms for the use of the laity, it was to Peckham's canon that people turned. Even the seventeenth-century puritans were indebted to him for their approach to Christian education, little though they knew it at the time. Peckham certainly had his faults, but his contribution to the life of the Church of England was immense and continues still. His Augustinianism would be recovered in the sixteenth century and form the basis of the classical Anglican formularies, and his attempts to demarcate the boundaries of church and state would set the tone for the development of classical Anglicanism into modern times.

John Wycliffe (c. 1330-1384)

No account of the pre-reformation church would be complete without some mention of John Wycliffe. As we have already remarked, he was long regarded as the 'morning star' of the reformation and the inter-denominational Wycliffe Bible Translators (founded in 1942) reminds us of what he is chiefly remembered for nowadays. Perhaps inevitably, modern scholarship has revised this assessment of the man and his influence, so that we are now more conscious that he was (like us all) a child of his time and only partially the harbinger of an era which did not emerge until 150 years after his death. It is relatively easy to accept that Wycliffe can neither be praised nor blamed for the English reformation, about which he knew nothing, but it is harder to swallow the fact that he almost certainly never translated a word of the Bible into English either. It is true that some of his followers did, and so it is not entirely misleading to call the two versions they produced 'Wycliffite', but Wycliffe was not a Luther or a Tyndale. The Wycliffite Bibles circulated in manuscript and were owned by some prominent people, but they were not published until 1850 and (as far as we can tell) exerted no influence on the classical English translations of the Bible which were produced in the sixteenth and seventeenth centuries.

Wycliffe's life was bounded by the university of Oxford, where he became master of Balliol College when he was still only about thirty years of age. He was completely immersed in the academic debates of his time and might have stayed within that rarefied world had he not taken up the cause of ecclesiastical poverty. He was upset that the church had so much wealth, although it was clear that the Gospels preached a life of renunciation of worldly things. He decided to challenge papal taxation, but unfortunately chose a bad moment to start complaining. King Edward III died in 1377, leaving the throne to his nine-year-old grandson Richard II, and soon afterwards schism broke out in the papacy. Wycliffe's enemies had little trouble getting him condemned, and popular agitation produced a Peasants' Revolt which frightened the already insecure secular authorities. Wycliffe had to withdraw from Oxford and was fortunate to die in his bed at the end of 1384. His legacy was swept away in 1407, when his beloved university was examined for heresy and measures were taken to ensure that nothing like his doctrines would ever resurface. Clergy today who have their licences revoked ultimately have Wycliffe and his Lollard followers to thank for this, since preaching licences were first introduced as a curb on their activities. Translating the Scriptures into English was made a crime, with the result that at the time of the reformation, England was the only major country in Europe which lacked a vernacular Bible.

Yet for all his failures, Wycliffe's name lives on. At a time when the church was becoming increasingly clericalised and institutionalised, Wycliffe dared to reassert the primacy of its spiritual vision. To him the church was the body of those who were in a state of grace, who had been touched by the Holy Spirit and called to salvation. There was no essential difference between the clergy and the laity, for both belonged to the body of Christ, who ruled over his church as its only true head and king. Priests, bishops and popes had a role to play in governing Christ's body on earth, but this was purely functional and did not give them any special status or privileges. If they failed to do their job properly, they not only could be deposed – they should be, for the sake of the health of the whole body. If they expected others to obey them, then they must earn that obedience. Here we see what would become an authentically Anglican approach to church hierarchy and government, distinct from the clericalism so rampant in the Roman Catholic and Eastern Orthodox churches. In this sense Wycliffe was indeed the morning star of the reformation, whose light was transmitted to his native land not directly, but through the witness of Jan Hus and Martin Luther. For although he was hounded and silenced in England, Wycliffe's writings struck a chord halfway across Europe. It had been many centuries since an Englishman had exercised such influence, but Jan Hus absorbed his teaching eagerly and through him it percolated down to the great reformers of the sixteenth century. When Henry VIII broke with Rome in 1534, Wycliffe was better known in Germany than he was in England, and it was from there that his voice was occasionally heard once more in his own country.

Wycliffe probably did not write anything in English himself, but he encouraged others to do so, and to that extent he may be regarded as the grandfather of English-speaking Christianity. What he certainly did believe was that Christianity was Christ and his teaching, all of which could be found in the Scriptures alone. This did not mean that he had a higher view of the Bible than his contemporaries, and it is probably a mistake to think that he restored the reading of it to the centre of the theological curriculum at Oxford. But he did believe that the Bible was the only legitimate authority for Christian doctrine, and here again he appears as the true morning star of the reformation. It was the Bible, and not some kind of philosophical or systematic theology, which lay at the heart of his preaching and teaching, an emphasis which remains characteristic of Anglicanism at its best. The chisel of modern research has scraped a good deal off the traditional portrait of Wycliffe, and to some extent he must appear diminished when compared with the image people had of him in the nineteenth century. But he left an enduring vision of a spiritually-minded church, ruled by the Bible and governed by people under its authority. The Anglican Communion today bears Wycliffe's stamp along with that of many others who came later and followed in his footsteps.

Thomas Cranmer (1489-1556)

Roger Beckwith

At one of the main road junctions in Oxford, where nearly every visitor to the city comes, there stands a monument erected in 1841, known as the Martyrs' Memorial. It commemorates the deaths at the stake of Bishops Hugh Latimer and Nicholas Ridley on 16 October 1555, and of Archbishop Thomas Cranmer on 21 March 1556, which took place nearby. Nowadays, on 21 March each year, a wreath is always placed on this monument, and the choice of date is significant. It is placed there not in honour of the graphic preaching of Latimer or of the penetrating theology of Ridley, but in honour of the pioneering liturgical work of Cranmer in drawing up the *Book of Common Prayer*. The light revision of it produced in 1662 is still used by many who love it, and forms the basis of numerous modern Anglican liturgies around the world.[1] Through frequent repetition, Cranmer's prayers have been impressed upon the hearts and minds of countless Christians down the generations. His theological legacy has been monumental, best seen in devotional expression, and his liturgies continue to mould Anglican identities today.

Appointed as Henry VIII's Archbishop of Canterbury, against his will, as early as 1532, it was Cranmer's uneasy role to be the main leader in the work of the English reformation. That the work was controversial goes without saying: the manner of his death shows it. And it was made more difficult by having to be done for the greater part of his ministry in joint-harness with so wilful and violent a monarch as Henry VIII, whose sympathy with reform was limited. Only in the brief reign of Henry's son, Edward VI, did Cranmer have vigorous royal support of an understanding and congenial kind.[2]

As a result, the judgement of historians and biographers on Cranmer has always been mixed. Those who disapprove of the reformation itself (like Eamon Duffy and Jack Scarisbrick, among writers of today) almost inevitably disapprove of Cranmer too.[3] He was trapped into various ambiguous and even dishonourable compromises which are easy to criticise, and it is undeniable that medieval religion still enjoyed widespread popularity. Those historians, on the other hand, who approve of the reformation and emphasise the corruptions of medieval church life and the positive influences of Lollardy and the Renaissance, are equally likely to praise Cranmer and to defend him, especially if they are themselves committed to the reformed Church of England. C.S. Carter and A.G. Dickens are examples.[4] There remain those Anglicans, of Tractarian sympathies, who look for the origins of Anglicanism in the seventeenth rather than the sixteenth century, and seek either to remould Cranmer on a Caroline model, or to dismiss him as a misguided forerunner of wiser spirits. W.H. Frere is an example of the former tendency and Gregory Dix of the latter.[5]

This confusion of voices has at least temporarily been silenced by the massive and perceptive biography of Cranmer produced by Diarmaid MacCulloch. The amount of fresh information which the author has unearthed or drawn together, after so long a period and so many previous attempts, is quite astonishing. And the straightforward and sympathetic, though not uncritical, attitude which he takes to Cranmer is appealingly moderate. Whether other attitudes to Cranmer will be able to reassert themselves, only time will tell, but for the present MacCulloch's estimate seems bound to hold the field. He explains that the archbishop

> attracted controversy and wildly polarized comment in his life and in the manner of his death. Ever since he was burned at the stake in Oxford in 1556, Thomas Cranmer's story has frequently been told in two completely contrasting ways: he has been portrayed as a hero or a villain. In either case, the narrator's prime intention has been to comment on a larger story, that of the Church of England: to legitimize the Church or to dismiss it, to present it as Catholic or as evangelical in character. There is good reason for doing this. It is impossible to disentangle Cranmer's career from the confused manoeuvres which led to the birth of one strand of world Christianity, the Anglican Communion. Cranmer's own reticence encourages this identification of his own story with the larger narrative of public affairs.[6]

The professor concludes, 'those who told the hero-narrative generally distorted fewer elements of the evidence than those who told the villain-narrative', but he resists the temptation 'to make Thomas Cranmer into either a hero or a villain; like most of us, he could be both.'[7]

Prominent amongst the many criticisms levelled at Cranmer are his involvements in Henry VIII's marriages and the trials of heretics. Both of these matters lay within the jurisdiction of the ecclesiastical courts, and thus involved the Archbishop of Canterbury. He annulled three of the king's marriages, probably with diminishing confidence in the evidence; and he had to condemn as heretics rash reformers, who pressed forward further or faster than royal authority permitted. Cranmer, with his belief in royal supremacy and his healthy dread of revolution and disorder, was unable to defend them, however much he might privately sympathise with them. But he was not cruel. His merciful character is shown by the fact that, almost alone, he repeatedly interceded for disgraced contemporaries facing execution – Sir Thomas More, Bishop John Fisher, the Princess Mary herself, the Carthusians, Anne Boleyn, Thomas Cromwell and the Protector Somerset. He was free from malice, courteous, quick to forgive personal offences, and only ready to punish wrongs against the king. He was a man of principle, and the liturgy he compiled reveals the religious basis of that principle: it shows him as a conscientious seeker after God and a humble believer in Jesus Christ.

The *Book of Common Prayer* was not his only gift to the Church of England, though it was the one that people got to know and love best. There were also his Forty-Two Articles, later reduced to Thirty-Nine, which made explicit the theology underlying his liturgical reforms. The Articles were mainly based on the Augsburg Confession of 1530 (though with a less Lutheran account of the Lord's Supper) and affirmed central Christian truths such as the Holy Trinity, the fallen state of human nature, the incarnation of God's Son, his atoning work upon the cross, the justification of sinners through faith in him, and the gracious operation of the Holy Spirit through the word and sacraments to impart this faith, along with repentance and love. The Book of Homilies, which Cranmer planned and helped to write, expounded the theology of the Articles and Prayer Book more fully and helped clergy to preach it. Four or five of the Homilies, those on 'The Reading and Knowledge of Holy Scripture', 'The Salvation of Mankind by only Christ', 'The True, Lively and Christian Faith', 'Good Works Annexed unto Faith', and less certainly that 'Against the Fear of Death', are thought to be Cranmer's own work. His controversial treatises on the Lord's Supper provide an important commentary on his liturgies; and he practically completed with the help of Peter Martyr and others a revision of canon law, the *Reformatio Legum Ecclesiasticarum*, though owing to Edward VI's early death it was not enacted. If the king had lived longer, the reform of virtually all aspects of church life might have been completed under his guidance. Cranmer did abolish the compulsory celibacy of the clergy, and led the way himself as the Church of England's first married archbishop. He also invited distinguished and judicious continental reformers to England, and if his plans for a synod of all the reformed churches had borne fruit, the subsequent history of Christendom might have been different.

As with the other reformers, continental and English alike, Cranmer's main allegiance was to the Bible, and to its gospel of salvation by grace, through faith in Jesus Christ. Because they were men of the New Learning, which had been brought into Europe by the Renaissance, they studied the Scriptures in the original languages of Hebrew and Greek, instead of relying on Jerome's Latin translation. *Ad fontes*, back to the source, was a key principle. Erasmus, the editor of the Greek New Testament, spent a significant part of his working life in England and the Great Bible of Tyndale and Coverdale, which Henry VIII in 1538 agreed to have placed in every parish church, was a fresh translation from the original texts.

Cranmer's explicit dependence upon the Scriptures is shown in many ways. For example, the language of the *Book of Common Prayer* is often borrowed directly from the Bible and was designed to harmonize with Tyndale and Coverdale's translation. Biblical authority can be quoted for every part of its spoken text.[8] The Articles also affirm the supreme authority and sufficiency of Scripture:

> Holy Scripture containeth all things necessary to salvation: so that whatsoever is neither read therein, nor maybe proved thereby, although it be sometime received of the faithful, as godly and profitable for an order and comeliness: yet no man ought to be constrained to believe it as an article of faith, or repute it requisite to the necessity of salvation.[9]

The purpose of the Bible in pointing to Jesus Christ and in strengthening the Christian is often expressed. It comes across clearly in his well-known collect for the second Sunday in Advent, at the beginning of the Christian year, which Cranmer personally composed:

> Blessed Lord, who hast caused all holy Scriptures to be written for our learning; grant that we may in such wise hear them, read, mark, learn and inwardly digest them: that by patience and comfort of thy holy word, we may embrace and ever hold fast the blessed hope of everlasting life, which thou hast given us in our Saviour Jesus Christ.

These themes are expounded at length in his 'fruitful exhortation' which opened the Book of Homilies:

Unto a Christian man, there can be nothing either more necessary
or profitable, than the knowledge of Holy Scripture; forasmuch
as in it is contained God's true word, setting forth his glory, and
also man's duty. And there is no truth nor doctrine, necessary for
our justification and everlasting salvation, but that is, or may be,
drawn out of that fountain and well of truth. Therefore as many as
be desirous to enter into the right and perfect way unto God, must
apply their minds to know Holy Scripture; without the which,
they can neither sufficiently know God and his will, neither their
office and duty. And as drink is pleasant to them that be dry, and
meat to them that be hungry; so is the reading, hearing, searching,
and studying of Holy Scripture to them that be desirous to know
God, or themselves, and to do his will.

Because the Bible is 'the food of the soul', Cranmer instructed his
hearers to

diligently search for the well of life in the books of the New
and Old Testament, and not run to the stinking puddles of men's
traditions, devised by men's imagination, for our justification and
salvation. For in Holy Scripture is fully contained what we ought
to do, and what to eschew, what to believe, what to love, and what
to look for at God's hands at length. . . . In these books we may
learn to know ourselves, how vile and miserable we be; and also
to know God, how good he is of himself, and how he maketh us
and all creatures partakers of his goodness.

With a catena of quotations from the Bible about the Bible, Cranmer
urged his congregation: 'These books, therefore, ought to be much in
our hands, in our eyes, in our ears, in our mouths, but most of all in our
hearts.' He concluded with a passionate call to feed upon the Scriptures
and put them into action:

Thus we have briefly touched some part of the commodities
of God's holy word, which is one of God's chief and principal
benefits, given and declared to mankind here in earth. Let us thank
God heartily for this his great and special gift, beneficial favour
and fatherly providence. Let us be glad to receive this precious
gift of our heavenly Father. Let us hear, read and know these
holy rules, injunctions and statutes of our Christian religion, and
upon that we have made profession to God at our baptism. Let
us with fear and reverence lay up in the chest of our hearts these
necessary and fruitful lessons. Let us night and day muse and have
meditation and contemplation in them. Let us ruminate and, as it

were, chew the cud, that we may have the sweet juice, spiritual effect, marrow, honey, kernel, taste, comfort and consolation of them. Let us stay, quiet, and certify our consciences with the most infallible certainty, truth and perpetual assurance of them. Let us pray to God, the only Author of these heavenly studies, that we may speak, think, believe, live and depart hence according to the wholesome doctrine and verities of them. And by that means, in this world we shall have God's protection, favour and grace, with the unspeakable solace of peace and quietness of conscience, and after this miserable life we shall enjoy the endless bliss and glory of heaven: which he grant us all, that died for us all, Jesus Christ: to whom, with the Father and the Holy Ghost, be all honour and glory both now and everlastingly.

The other central theme of the reformation, justification by the grace of God through faith in Jesus Christ and his atoning death, was expounded clearly by Cranmer in his homily on 'The Salvation of Mankind by only Christ our Saviour, from Sin and Death Everlasting'. He proclaimed:

Justification is not the office of man, but of God; for man cannot make himself righteous by his own works, neither in part, nor in whole: for that were the greatest arrogancy and presumption of man, that Antichrist could set up against God, to affirm that a man might by his own works take away and purge his own sins, and so justify himself. But justification is the office of God only; and is not a thing which we render unto him, but which we receive of him; not which we give to him, but which we take of him, by his free mercy, and by the only merits of his most dearly beloved Son, our only Redeemer, Saviour, and Justifier, Jesus Christ. . . . And therefore we must trust only in God's mercy, and that sacrifice which our High Priest and Saviour Christ Jesus, the Son of God, once offered for us upon the cross, to obtain thereby God's grace. . . .

Good deeds were necessary, of course, but as the fruit of salvation not the means to salvation: 'For that faith, which bringeth forth, without repentance, either evil works, or no good works, is not a right, pure, and lively faith; but a dead, devilish, counterfeit, and feigned faith, as St Paul and St James call it.' True Christian faith, insisted Cranmer, is shown not only by intellectual assent to the truths of the Bible and the creeds, but by obedience to the commands of Christ. Unless their hearts be 'harder than stones', those who reflect upon the 'great and merciful benefits of God' will be moved 'to render ourselves unto God wholly, with all our will, hearts, might, and power' and 'for his sake also, to be ever ready to give ourselves to our neighbours'.

The same emphasis is found within the *Book of Common Prayer*, and thus Cranmer made the doctrine of justification by faith alone in Christ alone the normative teaching of the Church of England. His communion liturgy lays great stress upon the atoning sacrifice of Christ upon the cross (as does Article 31). Standing before the Lord's Table, the minister prays:

> Almighty God, our heavenly Father, which of thy tender mercy didst give thine only Son Jesus Christ to suffer death upon the cross for our redemption; who made there (by his one oblation of himself once offered) a full, perfect and sufficient sacrifice, oblation and satisfaction for the sins of the whole world. . . .

The 'innumerable benefits' of Christ's sacrifice on Calvary are appropriated by the faith of the believer, who must rely only upon the grace of God not upon themselves. Just before the congregation receives the sacrament, they pray (in words composed by Cranmer, based on the Canaanite woman's encounter with Jesus in Matthew 15):

> We do not presume to come to this thy table (O merciful Lord) trusting in our own righteousness, but in thy manifold and great mercies. We be not worthy so much as to gather up the crumbs under thy table. But thou art the same Lord, whose property is always to have mercy. . . .

This point is driven home by the prayer of oblation, now placed by Cranmer post-communion to show that good works are the right response to God's grace but not the grounds of it:

> And here we offer and present unto thee, O Lord, ourselves, our souls and bodies, to be a reasonable, holy, and lively sacrifice unto thee. . . . And although we be unworthy, through our manifold sins, to offer unto thee any sacrifice, yet we beseech thee to accept this our bounden duty and service; not weighing our merits, but pardoning our offences, through Jesus Christ our Lord. . . .

The communion service of the *Book of Common Prayer* has been famously described by Gregory Dix as 'the only effective attempt ever made to give liturgical expression to the doctrine of justification by faith alone'.[10] Ashley Null calls it 'the ultimate expression of Cranmer's vision of God's gracious love inspiring grateful human love'.[11]

Other critics, however, have been unimpressed by Cranmer's liturgical reforms. John Field, the Elizabethan puritan, derided the *Book of Common Prayer* as 'culled and picked out of that popish dunghill, the mass book'. This is because, alongside Cranmer's overriding commitment to Scripture, the archbishop also had a sincere respect for tradition. He planned the English reformation on German rather than Swiss lines, beginning from where people were and not from a theoretical starting-point, and altering the *status quo* only where there was a good reason for doing so. His Prayer Books included significant parts of the medieval liturgy, translated from Latin into English, where he judged them to be edifying and true to the Bible. Cranmer only pushed for change where the liturgy had gone astray from scriptural teaching, or was understood in an unscriptural sense, and even then antiquity often provided the best model for reform. The combined evidence of his controversial writings, his library and the parliamentary debate on the 1549 Prayer Book show that he knew the liturgical evidence of Justin Martyr, Tertullian, Cyprian, the *De Sacramentis*, pseudo-Dionysius, Isidore and other of the Fathers, the Liturgy of St Chrysostom, the Mozarabic Missal and the epicleses from the eastern liturgies. Yet the Fathers were no absolute norm for Crammer. As his *Confutation of Unwritten Verities* shows, he recognized faults in their teaching which were not to be imitated.

Cranmer's attitude to antiquity was set out in Article 34, where he explained that the modern church was at liberty to change long-established traditions, 'so that nothing be ordained against God's Word'. But he went on:

> Whosoever through his private judgement, willingly and purposely, doth openly break the traditions and ceremonies of the Church, which be not repugnant to the Word of God, and be ordained and approved by common authority, ought to be rebuked openly (that others may fear to do the like). . . .

A similar perspective is demonstrated in his short essay, 'Of Ceremonies, Why Some Be Abolished, and Some Retained', which was first published at the end of the 1549 Prayer Book. Cranmer argued that some traditions in the Church of England had grown

> to more and more abuses, which not only for their unprofitable-ness, but also because they have much blinded the people, and obscured the glory of God, are worthy to be cut away, and clean rejected: other there be, which although they have been devised by man, yet it is thought good to reserve them still, as well for a decent order in the Church, (for the which they were first devised) as because they pertain to edification. . . .

He complained that 'our excessive multitude of Ceremonies was so great, and many of them so dark, that they did more confound and darken, than declare and set forth Christ's benefits unto us.' Yet he observed:

in this our time, the minds of men are so diverse, that some think it a great matter of conscience to depart from a piece of the least of their Ceremonies, they be so addicted to their old customs; and again on the other side, some be so newfangled, that they would innovate all things, and so despise the old, that nothing can like them, but that is new. . . .

No one can 'reasonably reprove the old only for their age', Cranmer continued, 'without bewraying of [revealing] their own folly'. In fact, unnecessary innovations ought 'always to be eschewed' for the sake of 'unity and concord'.

Naturally cautious and a respecter of tradition, Archbishop Cranmer did not attempt to reform the Church of England radically at a single stroke. He was also a compassionate pastor, concerned for those who found change difficult. Therefore he proceeded by stages, seeking to preserve the spiritual unity of the church (alongside the national political unity desired by the Tudor monarchy). His first Prayer Book was 'a very godly order . . . agreeable to the word of God and the primitive Church', according to the Act of Uniformity, but it was replaced by a second book in 1552 'for the more plain and manifest explanation' and 'for the more perfection'. The possibility cannot be excluded that, had Edward VI lived longer, there would have been yet another stage of liturgical revision, though the evidence that Cranmer intended anything of the kind is confined to a rumour reported in *The Troubles at Frankfort* (1575).

Cranmer's *Book of Common Prayer* achieved a unique reputation in the Protestant world. In his preface, 'Concerning the Service of the Church', he explained that he sought to attain intelligibility, edification and corporateness by producing a single, simple liturgy in the vernacular in which the Scriptures are read and expounded in an orderly way, biblical teaching is incorporated throughout, words are audible, actions are visible and congregational participation is encouraged. At the same time the archbishop virtually created liturgical English. The language he chose was suitable to express ardent but sober devotion and serious but affectionate instruction. In pursuing these aims there were, of course, limits to what he achieved. Like other students of the Bible, he had his blind spots. Being confronted with a largely illiterate church, and longstanding habits of infrequent communion, he was not able to implement his principle of congregational worship as fully as he wished; and he had to carry simplicity to lengths which restricted variety and freedom, and sacrificed some of the riches of the pre-reformation liturgy. He curbed music and ceremonial to an extent which may have been necessary at the time, but was not permanently desirable. He made rather too much of exhortations. Yet, when all necessary deductions have been made, his achievement remains extraordinary.

Just over a century after Cranmer put the finishing touches to his *Book of Common Prayer*, a light revision of it was produced in 1662 for the newly restored Church of England, after the chaos of the Civil War years. Although the Caroline divines changed individual words and phrases which had fallen out of use or altered in their meaning, they left Cranmer's text and theology essentially intact. It remains one of the formularies of the church, both unifying and edifying. Cranmer is as truly the pioneer of the reformed Church of England as Luther is of the reformed church of Germany or Calvin of the reformed church of Switzerland. And, unlike Luther or Calvin, he sealed his testimony with his blood.

Richard Hooker (1554-1600)

Nigel Atkinson

Richard Hooker, presbyter-theologian of the Elizabethan church, has long held a reputation as the quintessentially Anglican theologian. Anglican that is, as opposed to Reformed – more committed to the use of reason than magisterial reformers such as Luther, Calvin and Cranmer. Hooker is portrayed as an exponent of a distinctive Anglican *via media*, a particular way of doing theology which is alien to the reformation's key principle of *sola scriptura*. This view has dominated Hooker studies since John Keble edited the *Laws of Ecclesiastical Polity* in the 1830s, in the early years of the Oxford Movement, though the consensus has recently been challenged. Keble aimed to show Hooker's distance from the Reformed centre at Geneva and his proximity to 'primitive truth and apostolical order'.[1] Other scholars have highlighted Hooker's theological debt to the Dominican philosopher, Thomas Aquinas, or the Dutch humanist, Erasmus, who were less than clear about the reformation principles of *sola gratia* and *sola fide*.[2]

At first sight, the interpretation of Keble and his successors has much going for it. Hooker frequently clashed with the early puritans, who were known for their avowed evangelical commitment. For example, in 1586 a storm of controversy erupted over one of his sermons while Master of the Temple Church in London. As a loyal Elizabethan cleric, Hooker attacked the Church of Rome on the grounds that it failed to administer the spiritual medicine of justification by faith alone, thereby depriving people of 'comfort' when 'overcharged with the burden of sin'. However, although this meant that the Roman Church was 'corrupted' and that the pope was a 'man of sin' and a 'schismatic idolater' it did not mean that all those who were members of the Roman Church and who died in that church prior to the reformation necessarily went to hell. Indeed Hooker argued that Englishmen in previous generations who died as Roman Catholics were not to be regarded as papists but rather as 'our fathers'. Although the Church of Rome was 'drunk' and 'Babylon', it was still a church – misshapen, no doubt, but still retaining the Scriptures, the creeds and the ministry underneath its errors and superstitions. Hooker concluded that the Church of Rome was still 'to be held and reputed a part of the house of God, a limb of the visible Church of Christ'.[3]

To many radical puritans, Hooker appeared far too indulgent of Roman errors and heresies. Walter Travers, his colleague at the Temple Church, sprang into action that same afternoon with a sermon that sought to highlight Hooker's lack of commitment to the further reformation of the Church of England and, by implication, to the reformation in general. Some puritans even doubted that the reformed Church of England was a true church, because it was reluctant to abandon episcopacy and to undergo further reformation along Genevan lines. They believed the Church of England must be made as unlike the Church of Rome as humanly possible, expunging all vestiges of popery that still remained. Indeed another radical puritan, Thomas Cartwright, argued that it would be safer for the Church of England to mimic Islam than Rome. After their initial salvos, Hooker and Travers were locked in heated theological debate at the Temple Church week after week and began to attract large crowds. Commenting on the controversy years later, Izaak Walton penned a memorable phrase that has bedevilled Hooker studies ever since: 'the pulpit spoke pure Canterbury in the morning and pure Geneva in the afternoon'.

So was there a yawning theological chasm between Hooker's Anglicanism on the one hand and Travers' Presbyterianism on the other? Was Hooker's way of doing theology at root less than evangelical? Again and again he pleaded his wholehearted commitment to reformed orthodoxy. In the preface to his *Laws of Ecclesiastical Polity* he insisted that he was not 'bending himself as an adversary against the truth' which his puritan opponents had 'embraced'.[4] Differences over ceremony and government did not necessarily signal a disagreement over doctrine. On the contrary, Hooker wondered whether the radical puritans could really claim to be the true inheritors of Calvin's mantle. By seeking to out-Calvin Calvin, they were in danger of deforming the church rather than reforming it. He insisted that just because he opposed Calvin's self-declared disciples, this did not mean he was secretly against the Swiss reformer himself. This chapter will therefore focus upon Hooker's theological method – his theological first principles – to see how closely he is aligned with the magisterial reformers themselves.

Hooker's puritan opponents articulated their disagreements in an anonymous tract called *A Christian Letter*, which claimed that in all of Hooker's books 'reason is highly set up against holy scripture', and the Bible's role reduced to 'supplement and making perfect' knowledge which has been independently obtained through autonomous human thought. This was a serious charge. The reformers who confronted the abuses of the late medieval church were adamant that nothing less was required than a complete reshaping of its theological contours. They believed the fundamental reason that the church had lost its way, was because it had become overly dependent upon Aristotelian philosophy – indeed Luther argued that a spiritually blind pagan philosopher was being used to shed light on Scripture rather than allowing Scripture to shed light on pagan philosophy. Thus, the puritan charge against Hooker was that he was still inhabiting the swampy, low theological marsh lands of late medieval scholasticism, and that he still needed to climb the doctrinal hill of reformed exegesis in order to breathe purer and more bracing air. In short, they were arguing that Hooker was still unreformed.

At this point it should be admitted that Hooker's detailed analysis of reason's ability and role is complex and does sound Thomist in parts. For Hooker was willing, like Aquinas, to claim that the whole of the uncreated and created order was ruled by a hierarchy of laws. Laws which govern the natural realm are known as 'nature's law' and laws which govern supernatural and spiritual beings, such as angels, are laws 'celestial and heavenly'. In both these cases, Hooker maintained, angels and nature obey God's laws almost 'unwittingly'.[5] They are bound to be obedient because they cannot do otherwise. But humanity stands in a unique relationship both to God and to the created order, as creatures made in God's image. We belong to the 'stuff' of this world and are subject to nature's inexorable laws – we need to eat, drink, breathe and procreate. However these natural laws, in themselves, cannot exhaust the meaning of humanity's existence. Created in the image of God, men and women are 'voluntary agents' – to them has been given a freedom denied to other creatures.[6] To be sure this freedom could be manipulated to live lawless and disobedient lives out of step with both natural and celestial law – a point often made by reformed theologians. But Hooker argued positively that this freedom could also be utilised by humanity to frame laws that were in accordance with God's will. The gift of reason could help them to live not in disobedience but in obedience, to discern God's will and live a life pleasing to him. Such teaching made Hooker's puritan accusers nervous. For if Hooker was willing to cede so much power to reason, where was the need firstly of Christ's death on the cross and secondly of Scripture?

In order to be fair to Hooker we must not make the mistake that the radical puritans made. Having decided on *a priori* grounds that Hooker was less than reformed, simply because he was not convinced of the need to expunge episcopacy from the church, his other teaching was treated with immediate animosity – even though Hooker expostulated that if the puritans simply took off their prejudiced glasses and read his work with the same benevolence with which they read Calvin, they would see that he was standing on the same doctrinal platform. Ironically, in his teaching on reason, Hooker employed that most reformed and evangelical of doctrines, clearly articulated by Luther and embraced by Calvin – namely the doctrine of the 'two kingdoms'. He argued that with the gift of reason, even worthy pagans such as Plato could deduce that God exists and that if he exists it is humanity's duty to worship him, to love him, to pray to him and to depend upon him. From this vantage point of acknowledging God, reason could also deduce that people are duty bound to love their neighbours as well. All this was within reason's ability, in the kingdom of this world. But crucially, Hooker insisted that reason could not go further. It could not discover the way to eternal life, since its default position 'logically pointed to works', which were powerless to save. On this basis, and in the spiritual kingdom, reason was broken, weak and fundamentally corrupt. Therefore, Hooker concluded, humanity stands in need of a 'supernatural way', which is revealed in Scripture.[7]

This distinction between the two kingdoms of grace and nature became a prominent feature of Hooker's mature theology and fed directly into his understanding of scriptural authority. As he weathered the accusations that he was not an authentic reformed divine, he came to see that the radical puritan demands for the Church of England to abolish episcopacy were grounded in a use of Scripture that was slipshod if not positively dangerous. The puritans were determined to advance the 'further reformation' of the Church of England, after the first wave of the reformation which had dealt with doctrinal abuses. On the grounds that the episcopate, as it functioned in the English Church of the 1590s, was a far cry from the purity and simplicity of the office during apostolic times, they trained the big gun of scriptural authority on the small nut of church order.

When Hooker came to realise the full implications of what was being proposed he became increasingly anxious. Years previously, in the first round of debate with the presbyterianizing puritans, the Archbishop of Canterbury, John Whitgift, had asserted the principle that the episcopal office, as it had been received by the Church of England, was a legitimate expression of church order because it was not contrary to any specific command of Scripture. But now the puritans asked not whether episcopacy was *contrary to* Scripture but whether it was *mandated in* Scripture. They believed the church was being obedient to scriptural authority if, and only if, it acted upon direct and positive scriptural permission. The idea that they could still be obedient to God so long as they were behaving in a way that was not condemned by Scripture indicated a more nuanced relationship with the biblical text, which they found profoundly unsatisfying.

While Hooker engaged with these puritan demands, he was forced back to a familiar argument. He saw that reason had different roles and different levels of authority, depending on the sphere in which it was put to work. In the kingdom of this world there was no need to consult Scripture on the building of roads or houses, for example. In fact, this would be a misuse of the Bible. Common sense and simple mathematical processes provide all the necessary information to complete the task. In Hooker's theology, Scripture had to be used in close relationship to 'that end to which it tends'. In other words, if the Bible was used to find direction in the minutiae of life – ranging from the ordering of the church to the 'picking up [of] a piece of straw' – the effect would be to destroy its authority in the very area where it mattered the most, the way to eternal life.[8]

This is the heart of Hooker's concerns. Some have argued that his view of Scripture was not the normal Protestant view because he rejected Scripture's omni-competence. But this argument only holds if it is assumed that the radical puritans represented mainstream Protestantism – which in Hooker's view they certainly did not. Hooker maintained that the Bible's sufficiency, authority and overarching thrust must not be diluted by riding roughshod over its principal purpose. If the church was to ransack Scripture in order to find justification for its actions in thousands of different areas the 'main drift' of the Bible would be obscured. Although it may seem that those who constantly turn to Scripture for direction in every area of life are those who respect it the most, this is an illusion – just as when 'incredible praises' are given to men, although it seems an 'honour' it is an 'injury' for it can only serve to 'impair the credit of their deserved commendation'. Hooker states in a crucial passage:

> The main drift of the whole new Testament is that which St John sets down as the purpose of his own history, 'these things are written, that you may believe that Jesus Christ is the Son of God, and that in believing you might have life in his name'. The drift of the old [Testament] that which the Apostle mentions to Timothy, 'the Holy Scriptures are able to make you wise unto salvation'. So that the general end of both old and new is one, the difference between them consisting in this, that the old did make wise by teaching salvation through Christ that should come, and that Jesus whom the Jews did crucify, and whom God did raise again from the dead is he.[9]

With this deeply Christocentric appreciation of Scripture, Hooker was reluctant to see the Bible used to justify a novel form of church government. Like his puritan opponents, he held to the plenary, verbal inspiration of Scripture and that it was infallible and could not be supplemented by 'uncertain tradition'. Yet that did not mean Scripture could be used to justify the dismantling of episcopacy. To use the Bible in this way would be to ignore its overall thrust and force people to neglect 'the light of nature, common discretion and judgement'.[10] To appeal constantly to Scripture over a myriad of everyday activities that need no express biblical warrant was, as far as Hooker was concerned, pastorally disastrous and therefore to be resisted.

In their desire for 'the reformation of laws, and orders Ecclesiastical, in the Church of England', puritans like Thomas Cartwright and Walter Travers were seeking to rebuild the apostolic church out of the ruins of its late medieval corruptions. Hooker believed this was a laudable aim, but was concerned that if their zeal extended into too many areas the end result would be not reformation but revolution. Naturally, as good Protestants, Travers and Cartwright sought to base their 'further reformations' on scriptural warrant and they were convinced that a plain, unbiased reading of the biblical text would yield presbyterian order. But Hooker asked: If Scripture so clearly taught the presbyterian case, why has this not been understood until recently and then only by a few? He saw this lack of consensus as a real weakness in the puritan argument, and reminded them that the Bible is a book given to the whole church and not just to individuals. It could be dangerous to read the Bible in 'isolation' on the simple grounds that the human heart is naturally proud and fond of its own inventions. Therefore an isolationist reading might not yield what the text is saying but rather what the individual wants it to say. In a scathing attack Hooker wrote of the puritans: 'when they and their Bibles are alone together, what strange fantastical opinion soever at any time entered into their heads, their use was to think that the Spirit had taught it them.'[11] The remedy for this socially dangerous way of reading the Bible was to remember that it had been studied in the church for 1500 years and no one, until that moment in time, had ever entertained the notion that it taught the presbyterian form of church government. Presbyterianism was a new and 'singular' opinion, and Hooker wrote:

> where singularity is, they whose hearts it possesses ought to suspect it the more, in as much as if it did come from God and should for that cause prevail with others, the same God, which revealed it to them, would also give them power of confirming it unto others, either with miraculous operation, or with strong and invincible remonstrance of sound reason. . . .[12]

So Hooker pleaded that where Scripture is at best silent or at worse inconclusive the safest course is to follow the teaching and mind of the universal church. There have been bishops since time immemorial, so it would be best to retain them:

> A thousand five hundred years and upward the church of Christ has now continued under the sacred regiment of Bishops. Neither for so long hath Christianity been ever planted in any kingdom throughout the world but with this kind of government alone, which to have been ordained of God, I am for mine own part even resolutely persuaded, as that any other kind of government in the world whatsoever is of God.[13]

In conclusion, Hooker's prominent battles with the radical puritans over church government and scriptural authority must not be allowed to warp our interpretation of his theological position. This quintessentially Anglican theologian stood in the mainstream of the magisterial reformation. His theological method was firmly rooted in the principle of *sola scriptura*, though he was often misunderstood at the time and since. Until the revisionism of the nineteenth century, his Augustinian-Calvinist credentials were widely taken for granted. Hooker did not believe the distinction between 'pure Canterbury' and 'pure Geneva' to be as sharp as either his puritan antagonists or his Tractarian advocates tried to make out.

Richard Sibbes (1577-1635)

Mark Dever

During the long reign of Queen Elizabeth I and her Stuart successors, as has been seen in the previous chapter, many hoped and prayed for a more thorough reformation of the Church of England. The church had been established as a type of *via media*, though a very Protestant one – in which the doctrine taught was clearly Protestant, but the forms included ancient ones more associated with Roman Catholicism. A network of clergymen arose – known loosely as 'the godly' or 'puritans' or 'precisians' – who wanted its practices to be more demonstrably rooted in the Bible. There was no official membership, but from the time of the Elizabethan Settlement in 1559 through to the civil wars in the middle of the next century, the puritan movement was powerful. During that period the Church of England was served by many ministers who loved the church, but who simultaneously desired to see her further purified. They regularly called for reform in requirements of its clergy, church practice and discipline. Amongst the most prominent leaders of this puritan network in the early seventeenth century was Richard Sibbes.

From what we know, Sibbes grew up in a Suffolk home that was unremarkable. He had a free school education in nearby Bury St Edmunds, then was given a scholarship to St John's College, Cambridge which became his home for twenty years, as he moved from being an undergraduate, to a fellow, and finally to be a senior fellow of the college. It was probably around the time he first became a fellow that he was 'changed', converted to Christ through the preaching ministry of Paul Baynes, puritan lecturer at St Andrew the Great Church. As Sibbes' life unfolded in Cambridge, he himself became a noted preacher in English (as opposed to Latin) both in the college, and in the town. By 1617, he had also become the preacher at Gray's Inn, London, where he resided for much of the year, attending to regular preaching duties there. In 1626 Sibbes was elected master of St Catharine's College, Cambridge and he held both this position and the preachership at Gray's Inn until his death in July 1635. His sermons, some of which began to be printed during the last decade of his life, continued to come forth in increasing number from the press for decades after his death, and have continued in print since then. Many have regarded them as among the finest examples of Anglican – and indeed Christian – devotional writings.

Richard Sibbes believed and taught that the primitive church had been pure, but that it had been corrupted during the 'dark ages'. He preached that

> The times vary, but not the faith of the times. The same fundamental truth is in all ages. . . . If there hath been a church always, there hath ever been a divine truth. Now it is an article of our faith in all times to believe a 'catholic church'. Certainly then there must be a catholic truth to be the seed of this church. Therefore we should search out what was that 'yea', that positive doctrine in those apostolical times of the church's purity, before it was corrupted.[1]

Corruption, for Sibbes, meant going beyond Scripture, especially in any way that would distort Scripture's meaning: 'Our positive points are grounded upon the Holy Scriptures. We seek the "old way" and the "best way". . . .'[2] As he went on to say, 'Men ought to suffer for the truth, and not, for base ends, deny the least word of God, because it is a divine sparkle from himself.'[3] In Sibbes' own preaching, he demonstrated his confidence that the Bible was God's word written. In his many sermons from the Song of Solomon, he explained what the Holy Spirit was doing in writing (that is, causing to be written) such a book. He would exhort the Christian to believe in Christ's promises set down in the word.

Sibbes referred to 'the canon of Scripture'[4] and believed in the inspiration and authority of the sixty-six canonical books. He called the Bible 'the Book of God'.[5] This confidence in God's authorship of the Scriptures is expressed in his famous sermons published as *The Soul's Conflict with Itself*: 'Therefore hath God opened his heart to us in his word, and reached out so many sweet promises for us to lay hold on, and stooped so low, by gracious condescending mixed with authority, as to enter into a covenant with us to perform all things for our good. . . .'[6] And again, 'There is no readier way to fall than to trust equally to two stays, whereof one is rotten, and the other sound; therefore as in point of doctrine we are to rely upon Christ only, and to make the Scriptures our rule only; so in life and conversation, whatever we make use of, yet we should enjoy and rely upon God only; for either God is trusted alone or not at all.'[7] When there was a matter of controversy, Sibbes could say simply, 'We have the Scriptures of God for it', and so end the question.[8]

And what was at the heart of the Book of God? 'Christ is the scope of the Scripture. Christ is the pearl of that ring; Christ is the main, the centre wherein all those lines end. Take away Christ, what remains? Therefore in the whole Scriptures, let us see that we have an eye to Christ; all is nothing but Christ.'[9] Sibbes saw the message of the gospel, the good news of salvation provided through the cross of Jesus Christ, as the central message of the Bible.

As Sibbes preached about the parable of the Rich Pearl, he presented Christ as that pearl:

> Christ . . . became a ransom for many millions that were in bondage, so as all the whole church hath interest in him, and every particular Christian hath such a part in him, as if one only man had been in the world to have been saved by him, Christ must have died for him. He was given by God to purchase our redemption; and not only to purchase our deliverance, but also to make us acceptable, and to fill us with other things that are good in him. We have all that we stand in need of here and hereafter; all our grace and comfort ariseth from him. . . . Furthermore, it [Christ] is such a pearl as frees us from all ill; nay, it is powerful to turn all ill to the greatest good.[10]

Sibbes referred to Christ's death for sinners as 'purchasing' them. This crucifixion of Christ worked great good: 'So sweet and powerful is the death of Christ, that it turns all things, even the bitterest, to the greatest good.'[11] He portrayed Christ as speaking to sinners reassuringly, 'Fear not sin, for I have satisfied for it.'[12]

Though Sibbes had a powerful notion of the effect of Christ's death, he did not want to be mistaken to be teaching a kind of universalism: 'when Christ is said to redeem the world, it must not be understood generally of all mankind.'[13] Using the language of federal (or covenant) theology, Sibbes would often refer to Christ as a 'public person', meaning that his actions had implications for people other than himself. Adam's actions effected all humanity; Christ's all the elect. What Jesus Christ did himself profoundly effected others. In one of Sibbes' last sermons, he referred to Christ's death and its intention and effect as 'his blood, which was shed for all penitent sinners. . . .'[14] This message rang through all Sibbes' preaching and publishing.

The years of Sibbes' ministry saw two competing visions of the Church of England. William Laud, Archbishop of Canterbury (and an opponent of Sibbes) presented a more tradition-centred view of the church. It was a culturally conservative vision, favouring the existing powers. Sibbes had an altogether more word-centred, gospel-centred, preaching-centred view of the church itself. Here is how he described the church in one series of sermons:

What is the reason, that in popery the schoolmen that were witty to distinguish, that there was little Spirit in them? They savoured not the gospel. They were wondrous quick in distinctions, but they savoured not the matters of grace, and of Christ. It was not fully discovered to them, but they attributed it to satisfaction, and to merits, and to the pope, the head of the church, &c. They divided Christ, they knew him not; and dividing Christ, they wanted the Spirit of Christ; and wanting that Spirit, they taught not Christ as they should. They were dark times, as themselves confessed, especially about nine hundred and a thousand years after Christ, because Christ was veiled then in a world of idle ceremonies – to darken the gospel and the victory of Christ – that the pope made, who was the vicar of Satan. These were the doctors of the church then, and Christ was hid and wrapped in a company of idle traditions and ceremonies of men; and that was the reason that things were obscure. . . . Now of late for these hundred years, in the time of reformation, there hath been more spirit and more lightsomeness and comfort. Christians have lived and died more comfortably. Why? Because Christ hath been more known.[15]

Sibbes even saw God's providence in this gradual dawning of the gospel noon-day sun:

As the sun riseth by degrees till he come to shine in glory, so it was with the Sun of righteousness. He discovered himself in the church by little and little. The latter times now are more glorious than the former; and because comparisons give lustre, the blessed apostle, to set forth the excellency of the administration of the covenant of grace under the gospel, he compares it with the administration of the same covenant in the time of the law; and in the comparison prefers that administration under the gospel as more excellent.[16]

Sibbes' optimism held even when political events seemed to be putting the century-old Protestant settlement at risk. Again, he said, 'let us seriously and fruitfully consider in what excellent times the Lord hath cast us, that we may answer it with thankfulness and obedience. God hath reserved us to these glorious times, better than ever our forefathers saw.'[17]

How could any self-respecting puritan sound so optimistic at a time of increasing trial for the godly in the land? Because fundamentally, Sibbes' vision of the church was a typical one for the magisterial reformers, men like Luther, Zwingli, Calvin and Cranmer. They are called 'magisterial' not because they were such masterful reformers (though they were that), but because they worked through the magistrates, the political rulers.

They did not try to disestablish the churches. And the common thread that Sibbes and these earlier magisterial reformers had was a commitment to understanding the preaching of the word as the heart of the church. Sibbes had an evangelical, gospel-centred, vision of the church. He said:

> the mark whereby this church is known is especially the truth of God. That is the seed of the church, the truth of God discovered by his word and ordinance. To which is annexed the sacraments and ecclesiastical government; but the former most necessary. And these three were typified in the ark; for there was the law signifying the word, and the pot of manna signifying the sacrament, and the rod to shew the discipline. Those three were, as it were, types of the three marks of the church. But especially the word. For that is the seed of the new birth. Wheresoever the word hath been published, and there hath been an order of teachers, and people submitting themselves, there is a church, though perhaps there might be some weakness in other regards.[18]

It is worth considering how Sibbes and other puritans understood evangelism. If the message of the good news of Jesus Christ stood at the centre of the church (as they understood it did) surely evangelism would be prominent. Yes and no. Evangelism as we think of it today was not something that would have come quite so naturally to the mind of Richard Sibbes. Born at a time and in a place where everyone was brought into the church in infancy, where God-parents took vows publicly for the infants, and where there was effectively no discipline, everyone was a communing member of the same established church. There could be few exceptions, exiles from other countries conducting services in other languages, but even they would be under the supervision of bishops of the established church. Jews were not invited back to England until Oliver Cromwell's time. There were the non-conforming Roman Catholics, and they were in a special category of needing to have the gospel defined and defended.

Of course, Sibbes was well aware that there were hypocrites in the church, those who were not, in fact, regenerate. But there was essentially no one who would openly deny the gospel, and therefore the idea of millions of people living outside of the church who needed to be evangelized was not part of Sibbes' experience. Instead, his ministry was one of faithfully and regularly in his preaching setting out the promises of Christ and exhorting his auditors to rely upon them fully and truly. He called them to live up to their vows (or those taken for them). Sibbes' evangelism took place chiefly in his preaching.

When Sibbes looked to the New Testament for the apostolic model of ministry, he saw there the centrality of preaching. It is 'the preaching of the word [that] takes away the veil from the things, and the Spirit takes away the veil from our souls.'[19] To those who objected that they could just stay at home and read sermons, Sibbes replied,

> Yes. But the use of private exercises, with contempt of the public, they have a curse upon them instead of a blessing. It is with such men as with those that gathered manna when they should not; it stank. Hath God set up an ordinance for nothing, for us to despise? Is not he wiser to know what is good for us better than we do for ourselves? God accompanies his ordinance with the presence of his blessed Spirit. The truth read at home hath an efficacy, but the truth unfolded hath more efficacy. As we say of milk warmed, it is fitter for nourishment, and the rain from heaven hath a fatness with it, and a special influence more than other standing waters; so there is not that life and operation and blessing that accompanies other means that doth preaching, being the ordinary means where it may be had.[20]

How was one to get true faith? By preaching: 'These follow one another by a necessary order, for "preaching" goes before faith. Faith is the issue and fruit of preaching.'[21]

If preaching was so ordained of God and so used of God, then it made entire sense for Sibbes to give himself specially to it. Though he had a natural stutter in his speech, he was regarded as a powerful preacher. When he had been the preacher in English for St John's College, townsmen filled the college chapel. When the town of Cambridge then contracted him to be the town lecturer for several years, they had to build new galleries in Holy Trinity Church (by public subscription) in order to accommodate the crowds. And again, in the chapel at Gray's Inn, his auditors were numerous. Courtiers and barristers, earls and students vied for places to hear him. Again, the seating capacity had to be enlarged, with a new gallery being built near the pulpit. Sibbes was not merely a preacher himself, but he gave himself to train preachers. For years he had taught students, many preachers among them, at St John's College. His public sermons had been the means of converting many, like John Cotton (later a prominent puritan preacher in New England).

Sibbes and his friends also came up with a plan to place preachers in key pulpits around the nation. In the Church of England of the 1620s and 1630s many were concerned about the growth in 'formalism', Sibbes among them. These were years of conflict over town lectures (public sermons paid for by local laypeople, outside the normal church services). Sibbes acted to promote the reform of the church throughout the realm by establishing good preachers, and the combination of wealth and zeal in his circles inevitably led to activity. The Feofees (Trustees) for Impropriations were formally set up in 1626 to acquire advowsons (the right to appoint preachers at churches). These twelve Feofees acted on behalf of a much larger group, collecting money, finding patronages for sale and arranging for the settling of preachers in these locations. Their mission was to purchase the right to name the minister at various strategically placed churches. Sibbes was one of the original Feofees in this scheme, for which he earned the enmity of a number of clerics, not least Archbishop Laud.

In the midst of the uneasy and plague-ridden summer of 1630, Peter Heylyn, a fellow at Magdalen College, Oxford, attacked the Feofees for Impropriations in a sermon at the Commencement Act of Oxford University. Heylyn saw this as a dangerous move in form and substance. Formally, he may have quibbled with the means, but substantially, he disagreed with the clearly reformed agenda that Sibbes and his friends put forward in their vision of the church. As Sibbes asked, 'Where doth popery and profaneness reign most? In those places where this ordinance of God is not set up; for popery cannot endure the breath of the gospel. Thus we see the necessity and benefit of preaching.'[22] It was this 'necessity and benefit' that Sibbes counted as England's chief blessing and his own personal chief calling.

At the heart of Richard Sibbes' faith was his appreciation of his restored relationship with God through Christ. All the language about heaven, which is so prominent in his sermons, serves to turn our minds to Christ and enjoying his presence forever:

> From our communion with Christ, rising and ascending into heaven, and sitting there in glory, he forceth heavenly-mindedness, that our thoughts should be where his glory is, where our Head and husband is; and certainly there is nothing in the world more strong to enforce an heavenly mind than this, to consider where we are, in our Head. Christ, our head and husband, is taken up into glory. There is our inheritance; there are a great many of our fellow-brethren; there is our country; there is our happiness. We are for heaven, and not for this world. This is but a passage to that glory that Christ hath taken up for us; and therefore why should we have our minds grovelling here upon the earth? Certainly if we have interest in Christ, who is in glory 'at the right hand of God', it is impossible but our souls will be raised to heaven in our affections before we be there in our bodies. All that are Christians, they are in heaven in their spirit and conversation beforehand.[23]

And why? What was Sibbes' motivation in all his preaching and planning? Quite simply, the glory of God: 'Where there is a true judgment of God and religion, the soul of that man will never stoop to the creature; the soul so rejoiceth in God, as that it will not yield itself to any other. . . . In heaven we shall not be ashamed of things we now are ashamed of. A Christian soul is so ravished with the enjoying of God, that it mindeth almost nothing but him.'[24] Sibbes seemed to live such a ravished life. He was called 'the heavenly Dr Sibbes' and it was remarked that 'heaven was in him before he was in heaven.'[25]

In his last years Sibbes must have felt most keenly the limitations of his earthly hopes. The Feoffees had been legally dissolved. In 1633 the reformed Archbishop of Canterbury, George Abbot, died, and was replaced by Sibbes' opponent, William Laud. Older friends were passing away. Younger friends were departing the established church for congregationalism. During these years Sibbes could have easily despaired. But the source of his hope was Christ and his gospel, and of that he saw no reason to despair. As long as that gospel was preached in the Church of England, Sibbes would not depart. So it was that he remained until his dying day a member of 'the sacred communion of this truly Evangelical Church of England.'[26]

Robert Boyle (1627-1691)

John Coffey

In 1635, the year that Richard Sibbes died, Britain stood on the brink of an unprecedented upheaval.[1] This was not altogether obvious at the time. Some contemporaries later looked back with nostalgia on 'the most serene and halcyon' of all their days. Charles I was asserting his authority over his three kingdoms. Through Archbishop Laud in England, likeminded bishops in Scotland, and Bishop Bramhall in Ireland, he was busy reforming and realigning the national churches, promoting a high church drive for liturgical conformity and 'the beauty of holiness' in worship. The enemies of Laudianism were being routed. Puritan clergy were marginalised or even removed from their pulpits. In despair, thousands of the godly left for the Netherlands, the Caribbean and the new puritan colonies in New England. Parliament had not met since 1629, the press was heavily regulated, and outspoken opposition appeared limited.

The triumph of the Laudians was short-lived. For many Protestants, the Laudian programme constituted a betrayal of the reformation. There was much muttering about a 'popish plot'. The fear of popery was intensified by the aggressive Roman Catholicism of Queen Henrietta Maria at court, and by the Thirty Years War raging on the continent. To militant Protestants, the final battle between Christ and Antichrist was looming. Laud, who saw himself as a faithful Protestant, was widely despised as an agent of popery. His belligerent campaign to reshape the Church of England shattered its carefully constructed balance, dividing the English people and preparing the way for civil war. One very distinguished historian has suggested that Laud was perhaps 'the greatest calamity ever visited upon the English Church'.[2]

The crisis, when it came, quickly spiralled out of the king's control. In 1637, Scottish Presbyterians rioted in Edinburgh against the imposition of a new prayer book. A year later, they signed a National Covenant in which they vowed to defend reformed religion. The Covenanters went to war with the king, forcing him to recall the English parliament in 1640. Puritan politicians, like the Earl of Warwick in the Lords and John Pym in the Commons, orchestrated the repeal of the policies of the previous decade, and pushed for 'further reformation' in the church. Their drive for reform proved just as divisive as the earlier Laudian campaign. In 1642, the king was able to assemble his own party, the royalists, united by loyalty to the monarch and by fear of puritan innovation. The parliamentarian party was dominated by a core of puritan activists, intent on transforming church and nation. In the 1640s, they would remove over two thousand royalist or high church clergy from their livings. The puritans emerged from the first civil war (1642-46) victorious but divided. The Presbyterian majority favoured a policy of religious uniformity along the lines marked out by the Westminster Assembly of Divines, but the minority Independents enjoyed the support of the New Model Army. Led by Oliver Cromwell, they defeated the king in a second civil war, purged Presbyterians from parliament, executed Charles in January 1649, abolished the monarchy and the House of Lords, established a republic, and stamped their authority on Ireland and Scotland.

During the Interregnum (1649-1660), Cromwell and his allies strove to create a godly nation, even abolishing the 'popish' festival of Christmas. The Cromwellian national church accommodated a broad range of Protestants – Presbyterians, Independents, Episcopalian sympathisers, even Baptists – and there was considerable toleration for the puritan sects. But the *Book of Common Prayer* was officially proscribed, and the rule of the godly was widely resented. When Cromwell died in 1658, there was no one else of equal stature to lead the puritan cause. After eighteen months of political confusion, Charles II was restored to his throne.

The Restoration was initially welcomed by the Presbyterians, but it was to prove a disaster for them and for other puritans. Over two thousand were ejected from their parishes, as the royalist gentry took revenge for the civil war. Puritanism – which had been overwhelmingly a tendency within the Church of England – was now turned into Dissent. Thousands of Dissenters were imprisoned, and hundreds (mainly Quakers) died in English gaols. Yet the returning Laudians did not have everything their own way. Some puritan clergy – like William Gurnall, Ralph Josselin and John Wallis – remained within the church. Many nonconformists, like Richard Baxter (who had refused a bishopric), continued to attend parish services, and longed for reunion. While most of the leading preachers and theologians were now Arminian, some bishops and academics remained doctrinally Calvinist. Moderates, nicknamed Latitudinarians, favoured the comprehension of Dissenters, and even supported toleration. And the monarch himself combined a tolerant disposition with a dissipated lifestyle and Roman Catholic sympathies. His brother, James, Duke of York, even converted to Roman Catholicism, and rumours about his 'Popish Plot' to reconvert Britain led to a campaign to exclude him from the succession. Political parties emerged – the Whigs favouring exclusion for the Duke and toleration for Dissenters, while the Tories supported James's claim to the throne, and billed themselves the party of 'Church and King'. Yet even the Tories could not stomach the policies of James when he became king in 1685. Riding roughshod over Protestant opinion, he alienated his subjects, and was forced out of the country in 1688 by the Dutch invasion, led by William of Orange and sponsored by leading aristocrats and bishops. The so-called Glorious Revolution secured the Protestant succession, and delivered toleration for Dissenters. Hopes of reunion, however, were dashed.

Robert Boyle (1627-1691) lived right through England's troubles. He is known today as 'the father of modern chemistry', the author of 'Boyle's Law', and one of the chief pioneers of the experimental scientific method. Yet in his own day, he was also famous as a lay theologian and a leading apologist for Christianity. He was the author of some forty books containing three million words, and approximately half of his published writings addressed matters theological. And throughout his adult life, he was a faithful communicant member of the Church of England, a man renowned for his piety. Boyle's life is a window onto an era of political, ecclesiastical and intellectual tumult. He provides a perspective on a Church of England in which the centre failed to hold. And he helps us to see how Christian intellectuals reacted to the challenges of the new science and sceptical philosophy.

Boyle was the fourteenth child (and the seventh son) of Richard Boyle, the first Earl of Cork (1566-1643), a man who rose from modest beginnings to become one of the wealthiest members of the Anglo-Irish nobility. Richard Boyle was a convinced Protestant who credited his own rise to divine providence, but he was also driven by worldly ambition, and several of his children were notably dissolute. Robert Boyle was different. Sent to Eton College at the age of eight, he had several close shaves with death, narrowly escaping the collapse of a wall and drowning in a flood. He was convinced that God had preserved his life. In 1639, he was sent on a grand tour of continental Europe under the guardianship of the Huguenot scholar, Isaac Marcombes. He stayed for two years in Calvinist Geneva, reading Calvin's catechism on a daily basis. He was already displaying the voracious intellectual appetite that would characterise his entire life, devouring works of ethics, history and philosophy.

But the most formative event of these years occurred during a terrifying thunderstorm. According to his own autobiographical account (written in the third person), Boyle was 'suddenly waked in a Fright' with 'loud Claps of Thunder', 'preceded and attended with Flashes of lightning so numerous & so dazzling', that he 'began to imagine them the Sallyes of that Fire that must consume the World'. Fearing that the Day of Judgement was at hand, and considering 'his Unpreparednesse to welcome it; & the hideousnesse of being surprised by it in an unfit Condition', Boyle vowed that if he survived, 'all further additions to his life shud be more Religiously and watchfully employ'd'. When the morning came, with 'a serener, cloudlesse sky', 'he ratify'd his Determination so solemnly that from that Day he dated his Conversion'.[3]

Boyle's conversion experience, so reminiscent of the young Luther's vow to St Anne during another thunderstorm in 1505, was to mark him for life. The leading historian of his career has written that 'the central fact of Boyle's life from his adolescence onwards was his deep piety'.[4] As Bishop Gilbert Burnet emphasised in his funeral sermon, Boyle was a man of unusual spiritual intensity:

> He had the profoundest Veneration for the great God of Heaven and Earth, that I have ever observed in any Person. The very Name of God was never mentioned by him without a Pause and a visible stop in his Discourse, in which one that knew him most particularly above twenty Years, has told me that he was so exact, that he does not remember to have observed him once to fail in it.[5]

Others reported that Boyle never once failed to observe 'the office houre of morning & evening Devotion'. He would 'affectionally admonish' friends of their Christian duty, and 'severely reprimand his servants, when he heard them use any rash oaths, or Indecent Expressions'.[6] His devotional writings, such as *Seraphick Love* (1659), were frequently republished, and much appreciated by both churchmen and dissenters. Richard Baxter commended his *Occasional Reflections* (1665) as 'exceedingly useful'. When Archbishop Ussher encouraged Boyle to learn the biblical languages in the early 1650s, he immersed himself in Hebrew, Chaldaic, Syriac and Greek. He enjoyed long conversations with Jewish rabbis about Judaism and the text of the Old Testament, and wrote a treatise on *The Style of the Holy Scriptures* (1661). Friends reported that he always came to church with a copy of the Bible in the original languages, and could recite whole passages of Scripture in Greek and Hebrew.

Boyle's piety was not untroubled. Traditionally, he has been depicted as an establishment man – comfortably conformist and self-assured. But recent work on his manuscripts reveals a far more complicated soul – intensely scrupulous, obsessive, even tortured. Soon after his conversion, he was assailed by religious doubts, doubts he would wrestle with until his dying days. But he learned to live with his questions, and to see them as part of the life of faith. His personal struggles help to explain his passion for apologetics, for he felt the force of the new intellectual challenges to Christianity, and saw the need to grapple with them. Throughout his life, he displayed deep moral seriousness. His earliest writing project was a treatise on virtue, and he was generous to a fault with both his money and his medicines. At various points in his life he raised cases of conscience with spiritual advisors like Thomas Barlow, discussing them at great length. He had acute scruples about swearing vows and oaths, and it was for this reason that he refused the presidency of the Royal Society in 1680. As he faced death, he met with the clergymen Gilbert Burnet and Edward Stillingfleet to address his conscientious worries over financial affairs and blasphemous thoughts. He even feared that he had committed the unforgiveable sin – the sin against the Holy Ghost.[7]

Despite this spiritual and moral intensity – or perhaps because of it – Boyle was a man of broad sympathies. When he returned from his grand tour in 1644, England was in the midst of civil war. Initially, he considered joining the royalist armies, but he was dissuaded by his sister Katherine, Lady Ranelagh, who lived in London and hosted a salon for leading parliamentarian intellectuals, including the poet and pamphleteer John Milton. During the 1640s and 1650s, Boyle and Katherine were to be closely associated with the scientific projects of the Hartlib Circle, which gathered around the German Calvinist Samuel Hartlib and the ecumenical Westminster divine, John Dury. Another sister, Mary, had married the son of the Earl of Warwick, one of the most powerful puritan noblemen. Mary herself kept a remarkable spiritual diary, one of the prime examples of that distinctive puritan genre. Boyle dedicated two of his devotional books to his godly sisters, and met with them for spiritual conversation. But for all his puritan connections, he steered clear of partisan politics, and cultivated a wide circle of friends. Among his mentors he counted the great Irish archbishop, James Ussher, whose own political allegiance was very ambiguous. In the 1650s, his scientific work in Oxford involved collaboration with Anglican royalists like Thomas Willis and Christopher Wren.

Boyle prized peace and toleration. As the first civil war drew to a close in 1646, he expressed amazement that 'reasonable creatures, that call themselves Christians, should delight in such an unnatural thing as

war'. Three years later he wrote to his brother (fighting against the Irish
Catholics) that 'tho a Lawrell Crowne were more glorious amongst the
Romans; the Myrtle Coronet (that Crown'd bloodless Victories) ought
to be acceptable to a Christian, who is . . . to be very tender of spilling
their Bloud, for whom Christ shedd his'. Whilst he lamented the rapid
growth of sectarianism, he firmly opposed attempts to enforce religious
conformity. He approved of Dury's efforts to promote reconciliation
among the warring 'parties' of the Protestant world, and had high hopes
for 'the Advancement of Divinity'. Not much could be expected of 'the
Giddy Multitude' and those 'enslav'd to Factions and Interests', but 'the
Generality of inquisitive, intelligent and moderate Persons' were making
real progress in understanding the Scriptures.[8]

At the Restoration, Boyle conformed to the established church, but
he turned down the offer of a bishopric on the grounds that this was not
his calling. He also commissioned his friends Thomas Barlow and Sir
Peter Pett to write treatises in favour of toleration and a generous church
settlement. These hopes were dashed by the Restoration parliament,
and Boyle clearly regretted the expulsion of the puritans. His early
biographers agree that he abhorred persecution. He maintained friendly
relations with leading nonconformist divines like Richard Baxter and
John Howe and with puritan New Englanders like John Winthrop Jr
and the missionary John Eliot. Yet he also numbered several bishops
among his closest confidants, including the Calvinist Barlow, and the
Latitudinarians Burnet and Stillingfleet.

Throughout his career, Boyle downplayed the things that divided
Christians, and emphasised what united them. Like Richard Baxter, he
was an advocate of mere Christianity. He was, of course, a firm Protestant,
and a sponsor of Gilbert Burnet's *History of the Reformation of the
Church of England* (1679). But in contrast to many of his contemporaries,
his writings were not peppered with fierce anti-Catholic invective. He
disapproved of the charismatic excesses and theological novelties of the
sects, but was not in favour of blasphemy ordinances and heresy laws.
In his theological works, he studiously avoided doctrinal polemics, and
concentrated instead on defending Christian theism against atheists
and materialists. As a result, his theological writings are an exercise in
ground-clearing rather than a rich exploration of the central mysteries
of the faith – Trinity, Incarnation, Atonement, Resurrection – such
as one finds in the Calvinist Dissenter John Owen, or the Anglican
Arminian Isaac Barrow. But in significant ways, Boyle's writings laid
the groundwork for a defence of basic Christian orthodoxy.

Boyle endeavoured to give a reasoned defence of the faith while
recognising the dangers of intellectual pride. His exploration of

reason and revelation was a central theme in various works: *The Excellency of Theology compared with Natural Philosophy* (1674), *The Reconcileableness of Reason and Religion* (1675), *A Discourse of Things above Reason* (1681), *Of the High Veneration Man's Intellect owes to God, peculiar for his Wisdom and Power* (1684), *A Discourse about the Distinction that represents some Things as Above Reason, but not Contrary to Reason* (1690). What is striking about these books is Boyle's admission that revealed truths might well seem to be above reason and even contrary to reason, precisely because the human intellect is exceedingly weak and fallible.

This stress on the limits of reason led Boyle to distance himself from both rationalists and dogmatists. On the one hand, he was suspicious of doctrinal dogmatists, like the Calvinist theologians who insisted that divine prescience was logically incompatible with libertarian free will. By contrast, Boyle was content to hold together these two apparently contradictory propositions, aligning himself with the Arminians, but provisionally, and on distinctly non-rationalist grounds. On the other hand, Boyle had little time for Socinians who rejected traditional doctrines on the grounds that they were irrational. Boyle agreed that human reason might not be able to explain the mysteries of the faith: how God could be three-in-one, how divine foreknowledge could be reconciled with human free will, how a virgin could conceive a son, how souls could survive without bodies, how the dead could be resurrected. But given the frailty of human reason, why should one assume that such things were impossible for God? Rationalist presumption should not be allowed to trump revealed truth. Christians did not need to resolve all their difficulties in order to hold onto the doctrines of the Trinity, the Virgin Birth and Incarnation, the Resurrection, or the Immortality of the Soul. This did not stop Boyle trying to present a rational defence of traditional doctrine – *Some Physico-theological Considerations about the Possibility of the Resurrection* (1675) is a case in point. But he showed far less confidence in the imperious power of human reason than many of his contemporaries. Indeed, as recent scholarship has emphasised, his instincts are closer to those of leading nonconformist theologians than to his fellow Anglican Latitudinarians.[9]

Boyle then, both reflected and resisted some of the major theological trends of the later seventeenth century. In contrast to Sibbes and the majority of Church of England theologians before 1640, he was not a Calvinist, leaning instead towards Arminianism. In his *Seraphic Love* (1659), he offered a strikingly impartial summary of the two views of predestination, and referred to 'The Godly of both Parties'. He explained that Arminians did not denigrate God's grace or exalt human merit. He advised his readers that 'the doctrine of [unconditional] predestination is not necessary to justify the freeness and greatness of God's love'.[10] Yet while he reflected (and approved) the trend towards Arminianism, Boyle was wary of theological rationalism, and had little time for the militant anti-Calvinism of some Anglican clergy. Instead, he downplayed the importance of this doctrinal dispute, fostering rapprochement between theological factions.

His irenic and conciliatory style allowed him to work with different parties for a greater goal: the spread of the Christian gospel. In 1660, he paid for the printing of Edward Pococke's Arabic translation of Hugo Grotius' famous book of apologetics, *De veritate religionis Christianae*. Two years later, he became governor of the Company for the Propagation of the Gospel in New England, a position that he held for a quarter of a century. His energetic fund-raising for puritan missions to the Native Americans earned him the admiration of the leading missionary, John Eliot, who addressed him as 'Right Honourable Charitable indefatigable nursing Father'. Boyle used his influence to press the New Englanders to be more tolerant towards their own dissenters.[11] His missionary interests did not stop there. He also funded the publication of a Turkish catechism and New Testament, and the translation of the Bible into Lithuanian. Later in his life, he was a keen supporter of projects to publish and distribute a Gaelic Bible in Ireland and the Scottish Highlands. His faith was vigorously evangelistic.

The dynamism of Boyle's religion meant that it was not sealed off from his science. He first became fascinated by the new natural philosophy in the late 1640s, convinced that it could be an ally for the Christian faith. In 1649, he established a laboratory at his home in Stalbridge, Dorset. Here he conducted chemical and alchemical trials with mercury and other substances, used the microscope to observe tiny particles, and started to collect an enormous range of data on the natural world. He travelled frequently to London to meet with other natural philosophers, before moving to Oxford in the mid-1650s to join the remarkable group gathering around the divine John Wilkins at Wadham College. Wilkins was Cromwell's brother-in-law, but his scientific circle crossed religious and political divides, as did his definitive preacher's handbook, *Ecclesiastes*, which went through repeated editions following its publication in 1646. It was in Oxford that Boyle first met and employed the equally brilliant Robert Hooke. In 1660, Boyle, Wilkins, Hooke and many of their associates became founding members of the Royal Society. Boyle frequently attended its meetings, and contributed to its transactions.

From 1660 until his death, he published a steady stream of influential
books, usually translated into Latin. Among them was *New Experiments
Physico-Mechanical, Touching the Spring of the Air and its Effects*
(1660). This recounted his seminal experiments with an air-pump or
vacuum chamber, which demonstrated the properties and functions of
air by studying the effects of its withdrawal, and falsified the scholastic
Aristotelian idea that 'Nature abhors a vacuum'. Boyle's air pump
was unique, but it quickly became standard equipment in laboratories,
and helped to make him an intellectual celebrity – the greatest natural
philosopher of his generation. He moved to London in 1668, where he
lived until the end of his life with his sister in her large house on Pall
Mall. Here he established a large laboratory, and received numerous
foreign visitors – travellers, scholars, virtuosi, ambassadors, even
princes. Boyle cross-questioned them about an endless variety of topics:
from Chinese characters to New England skunks, from Transylvanian
mines to Swiss poltergeists. All of these were recorded in his 'work
diaries', which reveal his insatiable curiosity about the natural world and
human culture.[12] For Boyle, as for many English scientists in the later
seventeenth century, the study of the book of nature was a thoroughly
godly pursuit. A few decades later, Bach would sign off his musical
compositions with the phrase, Soli Deo Gloria; in much the same way,
Boyle saw the work of experimental science as doxological:

> When with bold telescopes I survey the old and newly discovered
> stars and planets. . . . When with excellent microscopes I discern
> nature's curious workmanship; when with the help of anatomical
> knives and the light of chymical furnaces I study the book of
> nature. . . . I find myself exclaiming with the psalmist, How
> manifold are thy works, O God, in wisdom hast thou made them
> all.[13]

Boyle also believed that the new natural philosophy had apologetic
value. He was aware, of course, that some advocates of the new science,
like Thomas Hobbes, were using it to push materialist conclusions. But
in his view, the mechanical philosophy pointed in a different direction.
The title of one of his last books explained his conviction: *The Christian
Virtuoso: Shewing, That by Being Addicted to Experimental Philosophy,
a Man is rather assisted than indisposed to be a good Christian* (1690).
Whereas many theologians – both Roman Catholic and Protestant –
clung to the old Aristotelianism, Boyle felt that ancient classical thought
fostered irreligion. Plato, Aristotle and Galen had mistakenly reified (or
even deified) nature, treating it as an animate and intelligent force, 'a
kind of Goddess'. The new mechanical philosophy, by contrast, reduced

nature to its proper place. By removing intermediaries between God and the world, it underscored divine sovereignty over creation and made room for divine agency.[14]

If science assisted religion, religion could foster scientific enquiry. Boyle was a theological voluntarist, who placed heavy stress on the will, power and freedom of God. This emphasis had practical consequences for how one conducted scientific enquiry. Because the choices of the omnipotent creator were voluntary and free, rather than necessitated by eternal reason, the laws of nature could not be discovered by human reason working from first principles. Instead, the contingency of the created order meant that it could only be understood through empirical research. Boyle's scepticism about a deductive-rationalist approach, and his support for inductive-experimental science, owed something to Francis Bacon, but it was also stimulated by his voluntarist theology.

As well as being free to create whatever kind of world he willed, Boyle's God was also free to intervene in his creation whenever he chose. Unlike Descartes, Boyle denied that God was bound by the laws of nature. His voluntarism entailed a strong supernaturalism, and he was keen to demonstrate the reality of God's action in the world. Throughout his scientific career, he remained fascinated by reports of the preternatural and the supernatural, including witchcraft and healing. When the controversial Irish healer, Valentine Greatrakes, took London by storm in 1665-66, Boyle observed him at close quarters on more than sixty occasions. He obsessively recorded tales of the weird and the wonderful in his work diaries. Yet his fascination with the supernatural should not be mistaken for credulity. Boyle was a cautious man, ever alert to the possibility of fraud and self-deception, and he knew better than to rush into print with tall stories. His apologetical arguments are marked by subtlety and sophistication, and have received fresh attention in recent years by philosophers who compare him favourably to his friend and executor, John Locke.

Boyle lived through some of the most dramatic decades in English history, and survived to see some disturbing developments. In the history of the Church of England, he represents the centre that failed to hold. Boyle wanted a broad church, one that would accommodate puritans and their critics, but Laudianism, the civil war and the Restoration combined to kill that dream. From his conversion onwards, he lived to glorify God, but the late seventeenth century saw the rise of a Radical Enlightenment that rejected traditional Christian doctrine and laid the foundations for modern secularism.

Nevertheless, Boyle (and others like him) did much to limit the damage done by fratricidal ecclesiastical conflict and sceptical philosophy. His irenic orthodoxy built bridges between warring religious factions, and modelled an open kind of Anglican identity that could learn from and work with evangelical Protestants outside the established church. In his apologetics, he showed how the old faith could be compatible with the new science. Along with Locke and Newton, he was one of the fathers of the mainstream English Enlightenment – an Enlightenment that was self-consciously moderate, empiricist and Christian. In contrast to Locke and Newton and many later Enlightenment thinkers, he had an acute sense of the limits of reason, and was content to accept the mystery of the Trinity and the Incarnation. In his will, he endowed a series of lectures for the defence of the Christian religion against atheists, the so-called Boyle Lectures. These have been revived in recent years, reflecting the new vitality of science-and-religion studies.[15] Boyle scholarship is flourishing. His collected works have been republished in fourteen volumes, his correspondence in six volumes, and many of his manuscripts are now accessible online.[16]

Anglican scientist-theologians like John Polkinghorne and Alister McGrath continue to walk in Boyle's footsteps. Although atheist fundamentalists try to claim the Enlightenment and modern science for themselves, they fail to reckon with Boyle and with the religious commitments of many early modern scientists. Of course, the term 'scientist' was unknown to Boyle, since it was coined in the 1830s (as was 'Anglicanism', though 'Anglican' has seventeenth-century origins). In using such terms we can transport anachronistic conceptions into the past. Boyle thought of himself as a natural philosopher and a reformed Christian. But he can be fairly described as both a great scientist and a great Anglican.

Susanna Wesley (1669-1742)

Martin Wellings

Susanna Wesley has not always been well served by her biographers, whether admiring or critical. Soon after her death in 1742 her youngest son, Charles, writing in what Maldwyn Edwards calls 'the early flush of his evangelical conversion', penned a poetic epitaph in which he dismissed most of his mother's life of faithful Christian discipleship as 'a legal night of seventy years.' It seems likely that this harsh assessment came about because it was only in 1739 that Susanna testified in the approved evangelical form to an assurance that she was a child of God.[1] Susanna's views on child-rearing, born of much experience and unexceptional in the context of the early eighteenth century, have horrified modern educationalists: 'When turned a year old (and some before), they [her children] were taught to fear the rod, and to cry softly. . . .'[2] Biographers struggling to understand Susanna's middle son, John, have ascribed his iron self-discipline, autocratic temperament and clumsy (or catastrophic) romantic relationships with women to his mother's enduring and baneful influence. Thus for Elsie Harrison, Susanna turned the nursery of the family home at Epworth into a kingdom where she could reign unchecked, and it was not until John went to Oxford that he first encountered 'grace and loveliness' after 'the moulding of Susanna Wesley's unrelenting rule of life,' while 'neither Grace Murray nor anyone else ever really had a fair chance with John Wesley', thanks to his mother.[3] Where Susanna has escaped the censures of immature evangelicals, anachronistic educationalists and amateur psychologists, she has often been elevated into the uncomfortable status of the Madonna of Methodism, in which role her individuality has disappeared behind the Methodist movement's quest for exemplary biographies. Furthermore, as a woman of the late seventeenth and early eighteenth centuries, Susanna has tended to be defined in terms of the personalities, careers and preoccupations of her father, husband and sons. As historians have paid greater attention to women's lives and experience, however, Susanna has begun to emerge as a significant personality in her own right. A fine biography by John Newton and a critical edition of Susanna's writings by Charles Wallace have made her far more accessible to modern readers, and it is telling that the *Oxford Dictionary of National Biography* encapsulates her significance not as 'the mother of the Wesleys', but as 'theological writer and educator'.[4] This brief chapter will seek to explore Susanna's faith and practice, and it needs to begin by sketching her life and placing it in context.

Susanna Annesley was born in London in January 1669, the youngest daughter of Samuel Annesley and his second wife, Mary White. Samuel Annesley was a puritan divine of great learning and firm principles: despite his steady support for the parliamentary cause during the English civil war, his career was adversely affected by courageous public criticism of Oliver Cromwell. The restoration of the Church of England and the enforcement of the *Book of Common Prayer* after 1660 cost Annesley the valuable London living of St Giles', Cripplegate, in 1662 but he continued to minister to a Presbyterian congregation in Spitalfields, experiencing occasional persecution by the authorities, until his death in 1696. Admired by Daniel Defoe, Dr Annesley was described by his son-in-law, the publisher John Dunton, as 'the Saint Paul of the Nonconformists'.[5]

In her early teens Susanna decided to leave Dissent and to join the Church of England. The reasons for this remain obscure, although it is possible that Susanna was wooed by the eirenic Anglicanism of London preachers like John Sharp, John Tillotson, Thomas Tenison and Edward Stillingfleet. Remarkably there was no resulting breach in the Annesley family: Samuel bequeathed his papers to his youngest daughter, and Susanna began married life in her parents' home in 1688; her husband, the Revd Samuel Wesley (1662-1735), was also a Dissenting convert to Anglicanism.[6]

Accompanied by their first child and eldest son, named after his father and grandfather, the Wesleys left London in 1691 for Samuel's first living of South Ormsby, Lincolnshire. In 1697 they moved further north to Epworth, in the Isle of Axholme, and stayed there until Samuel's death in 1735. At times there were hopes of preferment – even hints of an Irish bishopric – but these proved unavailing, perhaps because Samuel's High Church and High Tory loyalties placed him out of favour with Whig politicians and Latitudinarian bishops. Thus the London-born Susanna spent most of her adult life in the solitude of the Lincolnshire fens, coping with her own persistent ill-health, raising a growing family of probably eighteen children (ten of whom survived infancy) and managing a household which was often reduced to straitened circumstances by the financial ineptitude of her husband. A conscientious and learned, but tactless and impecunious, High Churchman, Samuel Wesley found himself imprisoned for debt in Lincoln Castle in 1705, and antagonised his parishioners to the extent that the family's property was attacked and their home destroyed, probably by arson, in 1709. Samuel Annesley's papers perished in the Epworth Rectory fire, as did an autobiographical manuscript of Susanna's; the family, however, survived, and the dramatic rescue of the young John Wesley, 'a brand plucked as from the burning', passed into Methodist folklore.[7]

Susanna's marriage has been described by Charles Wallace as 'companionate', using a category developed by Lawrence Stone, and she defended her husband's honesty and integrity in a long letter to her more sceptical brother in 1721.[8] In 1725, however, she wrote to her son John that 'your father and I seldom think alike', and at intervals their relationship was tempestuous.[9] Two incidents in particular shed light on Susanna's character and beliefs. In late 1701 or early 1702 Susanna declined to give an assenting 'amen' to the family prayers for King William III. Although both the Wesleys had High Church and Tory convictions, Samuel was more prepared than Susanna to accept the Glorious Revolution of 1688 and to regard William as the lawful king; for Susanna, James II was still the rightful monarch. This quarrel led to a virtual separation, until William's death in March 1702 enabled a reconciliation (and ultimately issued in the birth of John Wesley in 1703). During the period of estrangement Susanna sought advice from the Nonjuring bishop George Hickes, who counselled her to 'stick to God and your conscience which are your best friends, whatever you may suffer for adhering to them.'[10] Ten years later, while Samuel was attending Convocation, God and conscience were again invoked when Susanna's family prayers in the rectory kitchen at Epworth attracted large congregations and induced Samuel's offended curate, Mr Inman, to complain to the rector. Susanna's robust reply to her husband's letters ordering her to desist persuaded Samuel to back down. Echoes of this encounter were heard in 1740, when Susanna checked John Wesley's instinctive move to silence Thomas Maxfield, the first lay preacher of the Methodist movement.[11] Obedience to conscience and respect for calling gave Susanna confidence to subvert male clerical authority, whether that of her husband or of her equally autocratic son.

After Samuel Wesley died in 1735, Susanna left Epworth Rectory. For the next seven years she stayed with her children, finally moving to John Wesley's London base at the Foundery in 1739. As a lifetime of unpublished journals, letters and treatises of advice, mostly addressed to her family, drew to a close, Susanna ventured into print with a defence of Wesleyan evangelical Arminianism against George Whitefield. The pamphlet, *Some Remarks on a Letter from the Reverend Mr Whitefield to the Reverend Mr Wesley, in a Letter from a Gentlewoman to her Friend* (1741), although anonymous, is likely to have come from Susanna's pen and it comprises a vigorous assertion of universal redemption against Whitefield's advocacy of predestination.[12] In July of the following year Susanna Wesley died, and was buried at Bunhill Fields in London.

In its substance and contents, Susanna's faith may confidently be located in the mainstream of Christian orthodoxy. Susanna recalled that in her teens she had briefly flirted with fashionable views which contemporaries labelled Arian or Socinian, and gave thanks for Samuel, 'a religious orthodox man', who helped her escape from 'the Socinian heresy'; her settled position as an adult was a staunch and committed Trinitarianism, which perhaps owed something to the teaching of Bishop Bull.[13] An exposition of the Apostles' Creed, intended for all her children, but addressed particularly to her daughter Suky, set out as 'the first principles of religion – that there is one, and but one, God; that in the unity of the Godhead there are three distinct persons, Father, Son, and Holy Ghost; that this God ought to be worshipped.' An important source for Susanna's exposition was John Pearson's classic work on the Creed, first published in 1659. In her own private meditations Susanna used Scripture and the works of Bishop Beveridge to refute the teaching of the Arians and Socinians about the Trinity and the deity of Christ.[14]

Next to faith in the Trinity, Susanna strongly affirmed the atonement as the answer to human sinfulness. Reflecting on 'the sufferings of the holy and blessed Jesus' on Palm Sunday 1710, Susanna recorded in her journal her meditation on the condescension of Jesus Christ in 'veiling his native glory and splendour with our humanity' before consenting 'to suffer a lurid, painful, shameful death that he might satisfy the justice of God that loudly called for vengeance on all the race of mankind, that he might purify and reinstate us in the favour of God and purchase eternal salvation for those that believe.' Susanna urged awareness of the atonement as a motive for Christian conduct in a letter to her eldest son, Samuel junior, later the same year, and was making a similar point in writing to John Wesley two decades later. Her reflection on Christ's sufferings 'to heal and save a creature that was at enmity against God and desired not to be otherwise' suggests a therapeutic strand in Susanna's understanding of the atonement, as well as a juridical or forensic interpretation.[15] It has already been noted that Susanna upheld universal redemption and attacked the Calvinistic theology of George Whitefield; when John Wesley was wrestling with Article 17 of the Thirty-Nine

Articles in preparation for ordination in 1725, Susanna expressed the conviction that '[T]he doctrine of Predestination, as maintained by rigid Calvinists, is very shocking, and ought utterly to be abhorred, because it directly charges the most holy God with being the author of sin.' For Susanna, election was founded on God's foreknowledge, not on an arbitrary decree. Herbert McGonigle traces the roots of John and Charles Wesley's distinctively evangelical Arminianism to their spiritual formation at Epworth, and to the beliefs inculcated by their parents.[16]

Susanna's letter to 'dear Jacky' in February 1731 also discussed the issue of the real presence of Christ at Holy Communion. While maintaining that 'surely the divine presence of our Lord, thus applying the virtue and merits of the great atonement to each true believer, makes the consecrated bread more than a bare sign of Christ's body, since by his so doing we receive not only the sign but with it the thing signified, all the benefits of his incarnation and passion!', Susanna also emphasised that 'however this divine institution may seem to others, to me 'tis full of mystery. . . . Indeed the whole scheme of our redemption by Jesus Christ is beyond all things mysterious.' This makes the point that although Susanna was an orthodox believer and a faithful member of the Church of England, quoting Article 19 in reply to the question, 'What is your notion of a Christian church?', the heart of her faith is not to be found in mere verbal or intellectual assent to creeds and articles.[17] It is more helpful to ask why Susanna held her faith and how she sustained and expressed it.

It has already been seen that Susanna's faith was rooted in Scripture. This was both a direct influence, shown in the texts cited in her private journal, and an influence mediated through the *Book of Common Prayer*, echoes of which are to be found scattered throughout her writings. The tradition of the church is also evident, for instance in her use of Pearson and Beveridge as sources and authorities, although Susanna does not seem to have been directly acquainted with patristic writers.

In her theology Susanna refused to acknowledge an irreconcilable conflict between reason and revelation. Writing to John Wesley in 1725 she set out an anthropology which defined 'the true happiness of man' as 'a due subordination of the inferior to the superior powers, of the animal to the rational nature, and of both to God.' In her private meditations she gave glory to God for creating human beings as rational free agents, and described 'the law of reason' in terms of 'these two comprehensive duties, the love of God and the love of man.' In her reflections on the programme of education planned for her children, Susanna drew on the writings of John Locke, and concluded that the instructor should 'do nothing unworthy the reason God has given you.' Reason, however, like every other human endowment, had been weakened by sin and therefore needed to be restored by grace: ''Tis true God did at first bestow on reasonable beings sense, perception, and reason, but sin hath so weakened these powers that, unless divine grace restore them and renew the mind, they are in a manner perfectly useless, or at least will not serve to the end for which they were given.' Human appetites and affections have become corrupted and need to be redeemed through God's grace and a disciplined and holy life. In both diagnosis and remedy Susanna anticipated John Wesley's intention for the Methodist movement as a community of believers seeking the redemption of their 'affections' through God-given means of grace.[18]

If Scripture, tradition and reason played an important role in Susanna's faith and theology, so did Christian experience, later a hallmark of Methodist spirituality. It is easy, but misleading, to caricature the puritan piety of her childhood as introspective scrupulosity and to dismiss the Laudian tradition of the late seventeenth century as stiff High Churchmanship devoid of emotion. In reality, both the puritan and Anglican schools exemplified a religion of the heart, in which love for God and personal experience of divine love were central, and such emphases were vital to Susanna's own devotional life. In a letter to the younger Samuel Wesley in March 1704 Susanna expounded the duty of a Christian, beginning with a brief creed and moving on to obedience to the moral law. She continued, however, with a discussion of 'the highest and most noble part of Christian life, which consists in loving God', declaring that 'to love the eternal ever-blessed God with the full power and energy of the soul is the principal duty of a Christian and the complement of Christian perfection and happiness.'[19] This was not simply a topic for instruction. Susanna's private journal affords ample evidence of her personal experience of God's reality, grace, and love, sometimes expressed in ascriptions of praise and wonder interspersed into the text. It is this living, vibrant and lifelong spirituality which makes Charles Wesley's reference to a 'legal night' so incongruous and inappropriate: in the privacy of her daily reflections Susanna knew and worshipped the triune God, Father, Son and Holy Spirit.

If Susanna's faith was grounded on Scripture, tradition, reason and experience, it was practised intelligently, methodically and practically. As a child and young woman Susanna had access to her father's extensive library, and she married and mothered notable scholars. She was well read in contemporary theology, in the classics of the Anglican tradition, and in spirituality – she was able, for example, to give her son John a considered and trenchant critique of Thomas a Kempis, while admitting that 'I've Kempis by me, but have not read him lately'.[20] In the *Letter from a Gentlewoman* she demolished Whitefield's *Letter to the Reverend Mr Wesley* point by point, taking no prisoners in biblical exposition or logical reasoning.

The place of Christian experience in Susanna's understanding of Christianity has already been noted. She cultivated her own spirituality through a disciplined daily routine, withdrawing from the family three times a day for prayer, self-examination, spiritual reading and meditation. Her reading ranged from a Kempis to the celebrated but controversial contemporary theologian and preacher, Dr Samuel Clarke, and from the seventeenth-century Cambridge Platonists to the Scottish Episcopalian Henry Scougal. The voluminous puritan Richard Baxter was a favourite author for Susanna, as he was for her father and for her middle son.[21]

Susanna's prayer, reading and reflection fed careful self-examination. Her journal shows the results of hard thinking on difficult subjects (like the Trinity), but also the dissection of her own motives, aims and anxieties. She recorded, for example, an experience of spiritual inconsistency, when a day of delight in God's love was followed by one where Christian conduct was suddenly and inexplicably difficult: 'How inconsistent is your practice with your profession!'[22] She was honest in describing the family's financial problems, though rebuking herself for covetousness and 'some degree of idolatry' in trusting the fruits of frugality and industry to provide for the household's needs.[23] In her practice of self-examination Susanna reflected the puritan piety of her childhood, and recalled her father's expertise as a preacher in addressing pastoral issues and cases of conscience.[24] It should be emphasised here that Susanna was not given to morbid introspection: her quarrel with a Kempis, mentioned already, derived from his belief that God intended some people to be miserable, a doctrine she described in robust terms as 'extremely in the wrong' and 'impious', almost to the point of blasphemy. Susanna's faith was serious, but cheerful; her meditations, whilst fully acknowledging human frailty and the need for constant and disciplined endeavour against temptation, breathe a positive spirituality, a confidence in God's providence and love, thankfulness for God's mercies and a belief that God's intention for the soul is 'freedom and happiness'.[25]

It is evident from her writings that Susanna prized Holy Communion, expressing herself 'heartily glad' in December 1710 that her eldest son had received 'the Holy Sacrament', 'for there is nothing more proper or effectual for the strengthening and refreshing the mind than the frequent partaking of that blessed ordinance.'[26] The roots of the strongly sacramental piety of the Oxford Methodists may be seen in Susanna's practice, and it is significant that her experience of assurance in 1739 came as she received Holy Communion from her son-in-law, Westley Hall.[27]

Susanna was very clear that saving faith went well beyond mere intellectual assent to dogmatic propositions, writing to John Wesley in 1734 that 'By faith I do not mean an assent only to the truths of the gospel concerning him [Jesus Christ], but such an assent as influences our practice, as makes us heartily and thankfully accept him for our God and Saviour upon his own conditions. No faith below this can be saving.' Her own faith was intensely practical. It sustained her in the demanding tasks of household management at Epworth, coping with the hostility of the parishioners, sickness and mortality within the family and the mercurial temperament and frustrated expectations of her husband. In the early 1720s she penned a frank description of the family's plight to her brother Samuel, a prosperous merchant in the East Indies. While loyal to her husband and defending him against her brother's criticisms, Susanna admitted that Samuel Wesley was 'one of those whom our Saviour saith is not so wise in their generation as the children of this world.'[28] Meeting daily expenses, keeping the household together and educating the children fell to Susanna, and this regular responsibility was augmented when Samuel was away from home, whether imprisoned for debt in Lincoln Castle or in London for meetings of Convocation.

Susanna brought to her exercise of child-rearing the spiritual concerns and methodical approach which marked her own devotional life. She instilled self-discipline in her children, encouraging honesty and advocating a balance between study and games. She composed treatises for the children, explaining the Apostles' Creed and the Ten Commandments, and she continued to correspond regularly with them after they had left home. Even as a fellow of Lincoln College and spiritual guide of the nascent 'Holy Club' in Oxford, John Wesley received letters of advice and direction from his mother addressed to 'dear Jacky'. As the children grew older she set aside time each day for conversation about their spiritual welfare, explaining to her husband during his absence at Convocation: 'On Monday I talk with Molly; on Tuesday, with Hetty; Wednesday, with Nancy; Thursday, with Jacky; Friday, with Patty; Saturday, with Charles; and with Emily and Sukey together, on Sunday.'[29] It is interesting to discover that this initiative in Christian conversation was prompted by Emily Wesley finding in her father's study an account of the Danish Tranquebar mission, reported to and published by the Society for the Propagation of the Gospel. Susanna was so affected by the report that she not only instituted weekly interviews with her children, but also developed the pattern of family prayers which attracted the Epworth parishioners and offended Samuel's curate!

Charles Wallace suggests that Susanna Wesley's faith may be understood as a fruitful combination of puritan, Anglican and Methodist strands, emphasising respectively conscience, reason and experience.[30] This is a neat synthesis, although it needs to be remembered that all three emphases could be found in all three movements, and that puritans, Anglicans and Methodists each found a place within the post-reformation Church of England. Susanna held firmly to the faith once delivered to the saints. Her thoughtful orthodoxy was vitalised by love of God, nurtured by a cheerful, courageous and methodical piety, and expressed in personal devotion and conscientious discipleship. Context and contemporary expectations circumscribed her sphere of activity to a large degree, but her faith enabled her effectively to subvert some of these limitations, and the legacy communicated through her children exerted an incalculable influence on the evangelical movement within and beyond the Church of England.

William Wilberforce (1759-1833)

Mark Smith

William Wilberforce, perhaps the most prominent evangelical Anglican of the early nineteenth century, was born in Hull in 1759, the son of a wealthy merchant with interests in the Baltic trade. The early death of his father in 1768 exposed him to evangelical influence via his aunt Hannah with whom he stayed for extensive periods during his childhood, but this was opposed by his mother and grandfather because they thought it dangerous enthusiasm. By the time he went to University (St John's College, Cambridge) in 1776, William was little distinguished from the other wealthy and sociable young men with whom he spent his time, though his friendly manner and conversational gifts were then and subsequently to win him a number of important friends including William Pitt the future Prime Minister. With an independent fortune and little interest in the family business, Wilberforce decided on a career in politics and was elected, at the age of only twenty-one, to serve as the MP for Kingston upon Hull. In the House of Commons he declined to be identified with any party and generally took an independent line though his close friendship with Pitt drew him towards support for the government after the latter became Prime Minister in 1783. In 1784, when he was elected as MP for the hugely prestigious county constituency of Yorkshire and increasingly recognised as one of the most compelling debaters in the House of Commons, Wilberforce was poised on the verge of a glittering political career. His religious views at that time seem to have been purely conventional and though he was a regular attender at his parish church in Wimbledon, he also rented a seat at Essex Street chapel – the church of Theophilus Lindsey – the leading figure in the nascent Unitarian movement.

All this was to change however in 1784-5, when Wilberforce went on a continental tour in the company of one of his former teachers in Hull, Isaac Milner now a tutor at Queens' College, Cambridge and a man with evangelical sympathies. Milner introduced him to religious books like

Philip Dodderidge's *The Rise and Progress of Religion in the Soul* and in the course of conversation seems to have moved Wilberforce towards a more serious view of religion. On a second continental tour in the autumn of 1785 William moved further in his intellectual conviction of the truth of the gospel and seems to have undergone a classic evangelical conversion experience. In the light of this he considered withdrawing from public life altogether in order to devote himself entirely to God but he was persuaded by a number of friends including William Pitt and John Newton – now established as one of the leading evangelical clergymen in London – that he might serve God best by remaining in parliament. By 1787 Wilberforce had found his way to the two causes that were to occupy the remainder of his life and famously noted in his journal, 'God Almighty has set before me two great objects, the suppression of the slave trade and the reformation of manners.'

Although less well known than his campaign to abolish the slave trade the second of these causes – the moral reform of the nation – was a significant preoccupation for Wilberforce and one that he pursued with considerable energy. Some of his activity was public – most notably persuading the King in 1787 to issue a royal proclamation 'For the encouragement of Piety and Virtue' and establishing a society (the Proclamation Society) to support and enforce moral reform. Much of it, however, was private – in individual acts of philanthropy and in his support for the educational and charitable activities of others. It is in the context of this programme of activity that we should place Wilberforce's most substantial published work, *A Practical View of the Prevailing Religious System of Professed Christians in the Higher and Middle Classes of this Country Contrasted with Real Christianity*. Begun in 1793 as a tract in response to what he saw as the dire state of religion in England it had grown by the time of its first publication in 1797 to a full size volume of almost five hundred pages. The book sold rapidly, going through five editions in its year of publication and being published in America in 1798. It was continuously reprinted in Wilberforce's lifetime and remained in print through the whole of the succeeding century. The *Practical View* reached a large and diverse audience both at home and abroad and while not all welcomed its message it is difficult to deny its impact. Though discursive in form and occasionally rambling and repetitive the book expresses compellingly both Wilberforce's passionate concern for the religious and moral health of the nation and his own deeply held convictions about the solution to what he saw as an impending crisis.

A number of themes recur in the book but the *Practical View* is first and foremost an urgent plea for a return to 'Real Christianity'.

In making this plea Wilberforce was addressing himself to a specific audience – the upper and middle-classes of late eighteenth-century Britain – the people from which his own social circle was drawn. This was a group that in overwhelming numbers professed themselves to be Christians and to accept the authority of Scripture and yet as Wilberforce moved among them he found, in many cases, that their religion was as superficial and conventional as his own had once been. It was simply not the Christianity he had discovered in the Bible – in his view, indeed, it was not Christianity at all. Significantly, in making his case Wilberforce chose not to expose the spectacular scandals that abounded in late Hanoverian Britain but to focus on the ordinary and the every day – the conversations that might be heard in any family circle over dinner or at a tea party or in a gentleman's club. He was thus able both to analyse the mores of contemporary society and at the same time present his analysis in a context immediately familiar to his audience:

> listen to the unreserved conversation of their confidential hours. Here, if anywhere, the interior of the heart is laid open, and we may ascertain the true principles of their regards and aversions; the scale by which they measure the good and evil of life. Here, however, you will discover few or no traces of Christianity. She scarcely finds herself a place amidst the many objects of their hopes, and fears, and joys, and sorrows. . . . But what more than all the rest establishes the point in question: let their conversation take a graver turn: here at length their religion, modest and retired as it is, must be expected to disclose itself; here however you will look in vain for the religion of Jesus. Their standard of right and wrong is not the standard of the gospel: they approve and condemn by a different rule; they advance principles and maintain opinions altogether opposite to the genius and character of Christianity.[1]

The superficial religion which Wilberforce encountered in the drawing rooms of polite society and whose poverty he lamented had two main components: a system of 'mere morals' and a vague reliance on the benevolence of God. On the one hand such religion simply became oppressive:

> Robbed of its best energies, Religion now takes the form of a cold compilation of restraints and prohibitions. It is looked on simply as a set of penal statutes; these, though wise and reasonable, are however so far as they extend, abridgements of our natural liberty, and nothing which comes to us in this shape is extremely acceptable.[2]

At the same time it also became lax, vague and dangerously optimistic:

> they really rest their eternal hopes on a vague, general persuasion
> of the unqualified mercy of the supreme Being; or . . . still more
> erroneously, they rely in the main, on their own negative or
> positive merits. 'They can look upon their lives with an impartial
> eye, and congratulate themselves on their inoffensiveness in
> society; on their having been exempt, at least, from any gross
> vice, or if sometimes accidentally betrayed into it, on its never
> having been indulged habitually . . . on the balance being in their
> favour, or on the whole not much against them, when their good
> and bad actions are fairly weighed, and due allowance is made
> for human frailty' . . . and sometimes perhaps in seasons of less
> than ordinary self-complacency, they call in also to their aid the
> general persuasion of the unbounded mercy and pity of God.[3]

The origins of this superficial religion, thought Wilberforce, could be
traced to a number of causes: the secure state of the religious establishment
bred complacency, as did the growing wealth of the country. The trend
in much theological writing from the middle of the seventeenth century
and most parochial sermons in the eighteenth had downplayed the
fundamental doctrines of Christianity in favour of its moral and practical
aspects. Most fundamental of all, however, the nation had simply ceased
to draw its religion from the Scriptures:

> The truth is, their opinions . . . are not formed from the perusal
> of the word of God. The Bible lies on the shelf unopened; and
> they would be wholly ignorant of its contents, except for what
> they hear occasionally at church, or for the faint traces which their
> memories may still retain of the lessons of their earliest infancy.[4]

To Wilberforce then 'Real Christianity' as opposed to its cold and
superficial substitute was Biblical Christianity and his method throughout
the *Practical View* was primarily to attempt to bring Scripture and
his own reflections upon it to bear on his readers: 'Let it be sufficient
therefore, to refer the reader to the word of God'.[5] What then was the
content of this Bible-based religion?

The most important issue Wilberforce sought to bring before his
audience, precisely because it was for him both the foundation and the
centre of Real Christianity, was the question of the true basis on which
human beings might find acceptance with God. The first step was to
expose the optimistic view of human nature he encountered among
professed Christians as shallow and unrealistic and to replace it with a
biblical account of the fundamental corruption of that nature:

From it we learn that man is an apostate creature, fallen from his high original, degraded in his nature, and depraved in his faculties; indisposed to good, and disposed to evil; prone to vice, it is natural and easy to him; disinclined to virtue, it is difficult and laborious; that he is tainted with sin, not slightly and superficially, but radically and to the very core.[6]

Such a view immediately exploded the notion that humanity might find acceptance with God on the basis of moral effort or an overlooking of minor failings – a sort of contract in which each party independently fulfilled a set of conditions. Instead such a radical disease required an equally radical remedy but this is precisely what the gospel offered since:

Christianity is a scheme for 'justifying *the ungodly*', by Christ's dying for them '*when yet sinners*': a scheme 'for reconciling us to God – *when enemies*'; and for making the fruits of holiness *the effects, not the cause*, of our being justified and reconciled: that, in short, it opens freely the door of mercy, to the greatest and vilest of penitent sinners; that obeying the blessed impulse of the grace of God, whereby they had been awakened from the sleep of death, and moved to seek for pardon, they might enter in, and through the regenerating influence of the Holy Spirit might be enabled to bring forth the fruits of Righteousness.[7]

The issue of spiritual fruit was also crucial in Wilberforce's presentation of Real Christianity, not only tactically – to avoid the accusation of offering cheap grace or of undermining public morality – but also because he saw it as of the essence of the Christian life. The superficial Christianity of contemporary society failed because it rested on an inadequate foundation – the righteousness of humanity rather than the atonement of the Saviour – but beginning with the right foundation it remained incumbent on the Real Christian, with the aid of the Holy Spirit, to press forward:

solemnly resolve, through his Grace, to dedicate henceforth all your faculties and powers to his service. It is your's now 'to work out your own salvation with fear and trembling', relying on the fidelity of him who has promised to 'work in you both to will and to do of his good pleasure'. Ever look to him for help: your only safety consists in a deep and abiding sense of your own weakness, and in a firm reliance on his strength.[8]

For Wilberforce, then, a firm grasp of the Scripture doctrines of human depravity, atonement through the death of Christ and the sanctifying influence of the Holy Spirit was central to Real Christianity. However, this grasp was not to be a matter of intellectual conviction alone but of the whole person – mind, body and affections. As Wilberforce saw it, the problem with the fashionable religion around him was not just that it was unbiblical and superficial but also that it was cold and ineffective precisely because it did not understand the true depth of the gospel. Real Christianity on the other hand was marked by a 'cordial unreserved devotedness to the glory and service of God' provoked by thankfulness for what God had done. For Wilberforce spiritual practice was measured at least partly by its capacity to build an affective relationship with God:

> Let us labour then to affect our hearts with a deep conviction of our need of a Redeemer, and of the value of his offered mediation. . . . Let us not be satisfied till the cordiality of our belief be confirmed to us by that character of the Apostle, 'that to as many as believe Christ is precious'; and let us strive to increase daily in *love* towards our blessed Saviour; and pray earnestly that 'we may be filled with *Joy* and *Peace* in believing, that we may abound in *Hope* through the power of the Holy Ghost.' . . . With this view let us labour assiduously to increase in knowledge, that our's may be a deeply rooted and rational affection. By frequent meditation on the incidents of our Saviour's life, and still more on the astonishing circumstances of his death; by often calling to mind the state from which he proposes to rescue us, and the glories of his heavenly kingdom; by continual intercourse with him of prayer and praise, of dependence and confidence in dangers, of hope and joy in our brighter hours, let us endeavour to keep him constantly present to our minds, and to render all our conceptions of him more distinct, lively, and intelligent. The title of Christian is a reproach to us, if we estrange ourselves from Him . . .[9]

Such closeness to God was to be cultivated by a frequent and attentive reading of the Bible and other spiritual works, by fervent prayer and meditation and by the services of the church. Music and singing, activities in which Wilberforce himself took great delight, were recommended as likely to 'excite the dormant affections and maintain them in lively exercise'. Wilberforce, though he cultivated good relationships with nonconformists, was a firm advocate of the Church of England, convinced that the doctrines of Real Christianity were to be found enshrined in its Articles and Homilies and that its Liturgy was powerfully expressive of those truths which promoted lively religion, though not all appeared to benefit:

> Would to God it could be presumed, with equal confidence, that

all who assent to ... [those truths] in terms, discern their force and excellency in the understanding, and feel their power in the affections, and their transforming influence in the heart. What lively emotions are they calculated to excite in us of deep self-abasement, and abhorrence of our sins; and of humble hope, and firm faith, and heavenly joy, and ardent love, and active unceasing gratitude![10]

Lively, affective worship, passionately engaged in, was not recommended simply from Wilberforce's own tradition and experience, but also because it was the pattern he discerned in Scripture:

If we look to the most eminent of the Scripture Characters, we shall find them warm, zealous, and affectionate. When engaged in their favourite work of celebrating the goodness of their Supreme Benefactor, their souls appear to burn within them, their hearts kindle into rapture; the powers of language are inadequate to the expression of their transports; and they call on all nature to swell the chorus, and to unite with them in hallelujahs of gratitude, and joy, and praise.[11]

The presentation of an adequate Anglican and biblical warrant for the place of the emotions in religion was also crucial because of the context in which Wilberforce was writing. In an age deeply suspicious of the religious fanaticism which was held to have contributed to the civil wars of the previous century, and correspondingly insistent on the supremacy of reason in such matters, Wilberforce's emphasis on feelings – 'the affections' – was bound to prove controversial. A large section of the *Practical View* was devoted to defending it and especially to arguing for a distinction between true religious affections on the one hand and the mere effects of imagination or enthusiasm on the other. Moreover, as Wilberforce insisted, while cordial religious affections were a clear mark of Real Christianity their force was not to be estimated purely by their expression, 'by the degree of mere animal fervor, by ardors, and transports, and raptures' since these might be simulated or be the product of a naturally animated disposition:

These high degrees of the passions bad men may experience, good men may want. They may be affected; they may be genuine; but whether genuine or affected, they form not the true standard by which the real nature or strength of the religious affections is to be determined. To ascertain these points, we must examine, whether they appear to be grounded in knowledge, to have their root in strong and just conceptions of the great and manifold excellencies of their object . . . whether they have got the mastery over the vicious passions and propensities, with which . . . they are at open variance . . . whether above all they manifest themselves by prompting to the active discharge of the duties of life, the personal, and domestic, and relative, and professional, and social, and civil duties.[12]

Real religious affections, then, like Real Christianity itself were to be judged by the fruit they produced. Indeed, Wilberforce's clinching argument for the role of the affections in religion was to appeal to a more comprehensive and holistic understanding of the transforming power of the gospel itself. Why should it be presumed, he asked, that God should have excluded the emotions, 'the most active and operative principles of our nature' from the service of religion? To be sure they were as radically corrupted by sin as the rest of human nature but for Real Christianity:

It is her peculiar glory, and her main office, to bring all the faculties of our nature into their just subordination and dependence; that so the whole man, complete in all his functions, may be restored to the true ends of his being, and be devoted, entire and harmonious, to the service and the glory of God. 'My son, give me thine *heart*' – 'Thou shalt love the Lord thy God with all thy *heart*': – Such are the direct and comprehensive claims which are made on us in the holy Scriptures.[13]

At this point we are close to the heart of Wilberforce's spirituality – for him Real Christianity offered a redemption that was complete and a relationship with God that should by grace and in the power of the Holy Spirit be at work to transform every part of his humanity into the likeness of Christ. But if God's salvation was complete and comprehensive so must be our response. Wilberforce's Real Christianity was no holding back Christianity, no compromise Christianity, a principle and a power from which no part of life, no passion or pursuit could be exempt. There could be no compromise with contemporary standards of morality, no attempt to serve two masters. There should be no preoccupation with temporal gain, with worldly business or with personal reputation for their own sake but only so far as they might serve the happiness of one's fellow creatures and the glory of God. Love of worldly admiration, argued Wilberforce, was in its nature essentially and radically corrupt; and duelling – a significant feature of contemporary aristocratic mores – came under particular censure as a prime example of putting the applause of the world before the manifest will of God. For each Christian, moreover, there would be an accounting – a judgement to be made of their stewardship of the gifts, the resources and the opportunities with which they had been entrusted. An awesome sense of accountability to God breathed through the whole of the *Practical View*. It provided the impetus for writing the book in the first place and fuelled much of the seriousness and the urgency with which Wilberforce assailed the superficial religion of the fashionable world. Britain as a nation and the British as a people must grasp again what was at stake in the judgement of God and the power of the gospel and must do so before it was too late.

Wilberforce's joy and gratitude and his overwhelming sense of accountability drove him both inward and outward. Inward – to the delights of closeness to God and also to anxious self-examination as he constantly sought to sift his own motives, to separate the fruits of the spirit from his own naturally amiable temperament, and to measure soberly his own growth in grace. The importance of such careful and repeated self-examination is a recurring theme in the *Practical View*. Outward – it impelled Wilberforce to a relentless pursuit of practical Christianity, 'vigorous and continual resolution, self denial, and activity.' 'No man', noted Wilberforce, 'has a right to be idle', and how much more so was it incumbent on the higher and middle classes to whom he addressed himself, to prove good stewards of their resources: 'where is it that in such a world as this, health and leisure and affluence may not find some ignorance to instruct, some wrong to redress, some want to supply, some misery to alleviate?'[14]

Real Christianity for Wilberforce was thus not only God's answer to the corruption of the individual human heart but also to the problems of the political community – the nation at large. The true malady of political communities, he contended, was selfishness and Christianity was directly hostile to such selfishness: 'Benevolence, enlarged, vigorous, operative benevolence, is her master principle'.[15] But in order to produce these beneficial effects – to promote a worthwhile and a lasting reformation of manners – the religion of the country must cease to be just an ethical system – a means of teaching the lower orders their duty. It must return instead to Real Christianity – the power of godliness and not merely its form.

The life that Wilberforce led both before and after the publication of the *Practical View* was a consistent attempt, whatever his personal limitations, to put his theological and spiritual convictions into practice. Both the man and his book exerted a powerful influence on many of his contemporaries including people who were, at least initially, instinctively opposed both to his theology and to his politics. The atonement-centred, single-minded, whole-hearted Christianity that he espoused became one of the most significant cultural forces in early nineteenth-century Britain as more and more people began to share Wilberforce's conviction:

> that our dependence on our blessed Saviour, as alone the merit-orious cause of our acceptance with God, and as the means of all its blessed fruits and glorious consequences, must be not merely formal and nominal, but real and substantial; not vague, qualified, and partial, but direct, cordial, and entire.[16]

Charles Simeon (1759-1836)

Alan Munden

> As to Simeon, if you knew what his authority and influence were, and how they extended from Cambridge to the most remote corners of England, you would allow that his real sway in the Church was far greater than that of any primate.[1]

So declared the historian and essayist, Thomas Babington Macaulay, on the far-reaching impact of Charles Simeon, fellow of King's College and minister of Holy Trinity Church in the city of Cambridge. Macaulay had been an undergraduate at Trinity College in the early 1820s, when Simeon was at the height of his powers, and experienced his magnetism at first hand. Many concurred in the verdict. Another contemporary summed up Simeon as 'this extraordinary man – extraordinary in his appearance, his manner, his piety, his zeal, and his success. . . .'[2]

Charles Simeon was born in Reading, educated at Eton College and won a scholarship to King's College from January 1779. His life changed dramatically early in his student career, after he was told he was required to attend a college communion service. In preparation he read *The Whole Duty of Man* and books on the Lord's Supper by the nonjuror John Kettlewell and Bishop Thomas Wilson. This reading deeply challenged and troubled him, distressed as he was by his sins, but it led eventually to spiritual awakening in Holy Week, as he later recalled:

> I sought to lay my sins upon the sacred head of Jesus; and on the Wednesday began to have a hope of mercy; on the Thursday that hope increased; on the Friday and Saturday it became more strong; and on the Sunday morning (Easter Day, April 4) I awoke early with those words upon my heart and lips, 'Jesus Christ is risen today! Hallelujah! Hallelujah!' From that hour peace flowed in rich abundance into my soul; and at the Lord's table in our chapel I had the sweetest access to God through my blessed Saviour.[3]

At the time there were few evangelicals in Cambridge and Simeon was isolated from Christian fellowship. However, he was sustained in his new found faith by his personal devotions and by the Liturgy of the *Book of Common Prayer*. Simeon remained in Cambridge for the next fifty-seven years, a figurehead of the nascent evangelical movement within the Church of England. Generations of undergraduates sat at his feet, whether in his church on Sundays or in his college rooms for one of his regular 'conversation parties'. Anglican clergymen, both young curates and senior incumbents, sought him out for support and advice. In an age of missionary societies, he was often to be found at their forefront. Yet it was as a preacher he was best loved, perhaps the most imitated pulpiteer of his generation.

Simeon as theologian

While Simeon admitted that those who called themselves Christians held a variety of views about religion, he made it clear that *real* Christians agreed about the fundamentals. The true believer 'feels himself to be a sinner before God; dependent altogether on the blood of Christ to purge him from his guilt, and on the Spirit of Christ to renew and sanctify his soul. The necessity of universal holiness, too, is equally acknowledged by all.'[4] These fundamental themes dominated Simeon's preaching and teaching throughout his life. He believed that the Bible presents Christ 'as the only Saviour, and the all-sufficient help of sinful man'[5] and that it was the duty of ministers 'to preach Christ crucified'.[6] Scripture made it clear that individuals need to be born again, but '*how far* the Spirit of God works, and *how far* the mind of man, is a point which no human being can determine'. The experience of conversion might be sudden (like that of Saul on the Damascus Road) but this was not a requirement. New birth was often a process: 'we require nothing *sudden*. It may be so gradual, as that the growth of it, like the seed in the parable, shall at no time be particularly visible, either to the observation of others, or to the person's own mind'.[7] However, it was clear that 'religion does not consist in mere notions, just or scriptural; but in a conformity of heart and life to the will of God.'[8]

In Cambridge Simeon preached regularly at Holy Trinity, often several times a week, and also delivered a number of sermons before the university, which gave him the opportunity to present his theological principles in a coherent way. He set out the 'plain and simple truths' of 'evangelical religion' in sermons like *Christ Crucified, or Evangelical Religion Described* (1811) and *The True Test of Religion in the Soul* (1817). Another set of university sermons was published as *An Appeal to Men of Wisdom and Candour* (1815), including addresses on the corruption of human nature, the new birth and justification by faith. In Simeon's view these sermons, together with those on *The Offices of the Holy Spirit* (1831), comprehended all the topics which he considered 'as of primary and fundamental importance to mankind.'[9]

Despite his clarity on the essentials of the Christian message, Simeon was convinced that 'there is not anything more injurious to the Church of God than a party-spirit.'[10] He was concerned 'to prevent bitterness in controversy, and the magnifying of non-essentials; to smooth down the asperities of conflicting opinion, and resist the pride of party views',[11] and believed that ministers should 'guard against adopting the shibboleth of a party, or the dogmas of any particular sect.'[12] While Roman Catholics had added material that was contrary to Scripture, some Protestants were equally guilty. Simeon particularly criticised those 'who, whilst they profess to reverence the whole of the inspired volume, wrest and pervert its plainest assertions, in order to maintain a system of their own.' This had introduced 'endless dissensions, divisions, and bitter animosities into the church of Christ. Men have adopted sentiments of their own, instead of submitting to be taught of God; and then they have laboured, by forced constructions and ingenious criticisms, to make the scriptures accord with their views.'[13] He preferred teaching that was more balanced: 'Some are always dwelling on predestination and election, others on faith, and others on good works: some on the sufferings of Christ, others on the light within. To give every truth its due weight and proper place, should be the endeavour of a wise and sober-minded Christian.'[14]

Simeon was particularly critical of those who reduced Christianity to a human system, but he agreed that Scripture possessed an inner coherence: 'There is no real opposition between one part and another; but every truth has its proper place in the system, and its proper use ... [and] were this mode of investigating the holy scriptures more generally adopted, there would be an end of almost all the controversies which agitate and distract the Christian world.'[15] He believed that the teaching of Scripture was a 'far broader system than either Calvinists or Arminians admit.'[16] It was his conviction that they were both 'right in all they affirm, and wrong in all they deny'[17] and were therefore partisan, acrimonious and exclusive. On the other hand he admired the Anglican reformers who 'faithfully declared to us the whole counsel of God.'[18] Simeon himself disclaimed all names and parties and took 'his religion from the Bible' endeavouring 'as much as possible, to speak as that speaks.'[19] 'I keep simply to scripture, and not to system',[20] he said on one occasion, for 'God has not revealed his truth in a system; the Bible has no system as such. Lay aside system and fly to the Bible; receive its words with simple submission, and without an eye to any system. Be Bible Christians, and not system Christians.'[21]

Nevertheless, early in his ministry Simeon contemplated 'forming his own school of biblicism',[22] and although it was never formally constituted, his influence over generations of future ministers created a recognised 'school of divinity'.[23] These 'Simeonites' were identified by their distinctive style of preaching, their loyalty to the Church of England, their commitment to the Liturgy of the *Book of Common Prayer*, and their doctrinal stance was that of the Thirty-Nine Articles and the Book of Homilies.

Simeon as churchman

In Abner Brown's estimation, 'Simeon had not only grasped the simplicity of Evangelical truth, but also the true principles of sound churchmanship . . . he was a loyal churchman, staunch and affectionate to the Church of England.'[24] This was shown by Simeon's loyalty to his diocesan bishop, respect for parish boundaries and the great value he placed upon 'our excellent liturgy'.[25] For Simeon the *Book of Common Prayer* had no rival: 'If a whole congregation in one of our churches entered fully into the spirit of our Liturgy it would be a brighter resemblance of heaven than was ever yet seen upon the face of the globe.'[26] His own devotional life and public ministry were grounded upon the Bible and the *Book of Common Prayer*, which he regarded as 'a composition of unrivalled excellence.'[27] It was his deep conviction that the Liturgy possessed 'a beauty and a holiness superior to what is found in any other church on earth.'[28] This perspective was brought home to his hearers in prominent university sermons such as *The Churchman's Confession, or An Appeal to the Liturgy* (1805) and *The Excellency of the Liturgy* (1811).

Simeon expressed his thankfulness to God for the formularies of the Church of England which represented 'the authentic records of the doctrines of our church.'[29] He viewed the Articles, Homilies and Liturgy as 'the standard of divine truth'[30] and 'an authorised exposition of the sense in which all her members profess to understand the scriptures.'[31] The strength of the Church of England was found in '*her Articles*, how plain, how strong, how scriptural . . . *her Homilies*, formed by men of God who knew what assaults would be made against her . . . *her Liturgy*, next to the Bible, it stands the wonder of the world. Never was there such a composition for the use of those who would worship God in spirit and in truth.'[32] Simeon had little sympathy for 'the novelties, and follies, and fanaticisms' which sprang up in the early nineteenth century. In the words of one contemporary, 'The advocates of tongues and miracles and voices and of the personal reign of our Lord found no support in him; any more than the high Calvinism on the one hand, or the Arminianism on the other which at different times threatened divisions in the church. [For] the moderation and comprehension of the Church of England was his joy.'[33]

Simeon provided a good role model for those intending to be ordained. As Charles Smyth observes, 'It was Simeon who, more than any other single individual, taught the younger Evangelicals to love the Church of England and enabled them to feel that they belonged within her body', and 'without the steadying influence of Simeon at Cambridge, there would have been many more secessions than in fact occurred.'[34] In his public ministry and private counsel, in parochial organisation and spiritual oversight, Simeon practised what he preached. So significant was he that Smyth suggests he ought to be put alongside Bishop Samuel Wilberforce 'as one of the founding fathers, or remodellers of the Church of England in the nineteenth century'.[35] Dean William Lake referred to Simeon as 'the regenerator of the English church'.[36]

Simeon as mentor

During his long ministry at Cambridge, Simeon exercised a powerful influence over generations of undergraduates, some of whom were to become evangelical leaders within the Church of England. Through their attendance at public worship at Holy Trinity, and in private discussion and debate in his rooms at King's College, they were grounded in his principles and practice. His personality and character may be seen in the testimony of three typical Simeonites. Thomas Dykes at first thought that Simeon was 'one of the most unlikely persons to become extensively useful that he had ever known'. Yet his mentor became 'an example of what might be done by a truly earnest Christian, for the formation of his own mind, for the improvement of his own talents, and for making them extensively useful to others.'[37] Another undergraduate, William Nunn, experienced something of Simeon's brusque manner and even his wrath. The preacher 'seemed very angry' when he discovered that Nunn had expounded the Bible extempore at an unofficial prayer meeting and threatened to inform the tutors at St John's College if it ever happened again.[38] One of Simeon's most influential followers was Francis Close, who had been converted under the ministry of John Scott of Hull, and who became closely involved with Simeon as an undergraduate. He recalled: 'In October 1816 . . . I presented my introduction to him. From that day until his death, he was my affectionate father, my generous patron, and my wise and helpful counsellor. There were few like him, a perfect gentleman, a deeply taught Christian and as such wonderfully instructed out of God's Word.'[39]

Simeon as preacher

Simeon preached week after week at Holy Trinity for over half a century, with only occasional breaks due to illness, incapacity and absence from Cambridge. He was conscientious in the preparation of his sermons. It took him at least twelve hours to prepare each address and he made use of the Greek text (including the Septuagint) and a wide range of commentaries and expositions. It was his goal to bring out the natural meaning of the text, and to ensure that his teaching was consistent with the Christian revelation. His intention was clarity and simplicity, and he aimed always 'to humble the sinner, to exalt the Saviour, and to promote holiness.'[40] 'The first object of a Christian minister is to proclaim the gospel of salvation',[41] and 'never forget', he said, 'that you have to win souls.'[42]

Simeon's own sermon preparation, his fortnightly sermon classes for ordinands and his *Helps to Composition, or One Hundred Skeletons of Sermons* (1796) all contributed towards his expertise. His published sermons were gradually expanded into a twenty-one volume work entitled *Horae Homileticae*, completed by 1833 and dedicated to William Howley, the Archbishop of Canterbury. It contained 2,536 sermons, an English translation of John Claude's *Essay on the Composition of a Sermon* and an extensive index. These 'short discourses on divers subjects'[43] were intended to be the basis for family prayers and to assist busy clergy as part of their sermon preparation. Simeon rarely read his sermons, but preached from notes which were subsequently written up to form the basis of *Horae Homileticae.* His advice to younger ministers was not to preach extempore until they had preached 300 to 400 written sermons. After discovering the *Essay on Composition* by Claude (a seventeenth-century French Reformed pastor), Simeon's own preaching had improved significantly and he taught Claude's principles in his sermon classes. He insisted that a sermon should contain three parts: the exordium, the discussion and the application. The opening (which was to be composed last) was intended to prepare the hearers for the sermon; the conclusion should touch their hearts; and the discussion should always be a clear exposition of Scripture, that would illuminate the text and not obscure it.

Alongside *Horae Homileticae*, Simeon encouraged the use of the *Prayers and Offices of Devotion* by the seventeenth-century divine, Benjamin Jenks, and he published several editions of this work. Jenks was a man after Simeon's heart – steeped in the Bible and in the Anglican tradition. Bishop Walter Shirley regarded Jenks' *Prayers* to be 'almost a cento of the Liturgy of the church.'[44]

Simeon as missioner

Simeon was directly involved in mission at home and overseas. He was assiduous in his parochial duties, dividing the parish of Holy Trinity into districts, and pairs of male and female visitors reported back to him once a month. Alongside this, twelve men supervised financial collections for the poor. He also divided the committed core of the congregation into six groups (separate for men and women) and met with each group once a month. Simeon gave his backing to the British and Foreign Bible Society, and supported the formation of an auxiliary in Cambridge in December 1811, in the face of considerable opposition. He also welcomed the establishment, shortly before his death in 1836, of the Church Pastoral Aid Society to supply evangelical clergy and lay workers for Anglican parishes.

Although he seldom travelled outside England, overseas mission was one of Simeon's chief passions. He was involved in discussions amongst the London Eclectic Society on the most effective methods 'to promote the knowledge of the gospel among the heathen', which led to the formation in April 1799 of the Church Missionary Society, of which Simeon was a key advocate. India became his special concern and he confessed that 'I used jocosely to call India my *diocese*. Since there has been a bishop [from 1814], I modestly call it my *province*.'[45] Through his influence in Cambridge, he was able to recruit dozens of young clergy to serve overseas, as chaplains to the East India Company and as CMS missionaries. Two of his curates and closest friends, Henry Martyn and Thomas Thomason, both made their mark in India.

The evangelisation of the Jews was another of Simeon's preoccupations, and he was so committed to the cause that a friend called him 'Jew mad'.[46] He is said to have remarked that the conversion of the Jews was 'the most important object in the world'[47] and many of his sermons in *Horae Homileticae* were on the theme of the conversion and restoration of the Jewish people. In Simeon's opinion, the 'Jews should be pressed with vital Christianity at once.'[48] This was not because he had any sympathy for pre-millennialism, but because the conversion of the Jews would have an impact upon the conversion of the Gentiles. Christians were also expected to give financial support to Jewish missions: 'If there be a collection in aid of their conversion, the audience might be urged to show the measure of their love by the extent of their donations.'[49] After the nonconformists withdrew their support from the London Society for Promoting Christianity amongst the Jews, Simeon became a prominent leader of the society. He was 'assiduous' in his attendance at the committee,[50] spoke on numerous occasions at the annual meetings, preached deputation sermons and encouraged the formation of auxiliaries in parishes throughout the country. He also contributed articles to the *Jewish Expositor* and frequently preached to Jews in London. At the laying of the foundation stone of the Episcopal Jews' Chapel in Palestine Place, Bethnal Green in 1813 he gave 200 guineas and on a subsequent occasion £1,000. In 1829 Simeon was one of the founders of the Operative Jewish Converts' Institution, which provided accommodation and employment for Messianic Jews.

Simeon as patron

Simeon's patronage extended beyond his personal support of individuals to the ownership of advowsons (the right of presentation to Church of England parishes). The establishment of patronage solved 'the problem of continuity' for evangelical ministry.[51] Between 1816 and 1836, Simeon acquired the patronage of twenty-one livings, some in watering places like Cheltenham, Bath and Bridlington, others in urban centres like Derby, Bradford and Liverpool.

In an age when livings were bought and sold as valuable real estate, Simeon made it clear that there was a difference between himself and other men who purchased advowsons: 'They purchase *income* – I purchase *spheres*, wherein the prosperity of the established church and the kingdom of our blessed Lord, may be advanced; and not for a season only, but if it please God, in perpetuity also.'[52] The standard by which Simeon judged the suitability of a candidate for a vacant living was clear. He must be 'a truly pious and devoted man, a man of God in deed and in truth, who, with his piety, combines a solid judgment and a perfectly independent mind.'[53] These principles where laid out in the charge to his Simeon Trustees (established in 1817):

> When they shall be called upon to appoint to a living, they consult nothing but the welfare of the people, for whom they are to provide, and whose eternal interests have been confided to them. They must on no account be influenced by any solicitation of the great and powerful, or by any partiality towards a particular individual, or by compassion towards any one on account of the largeness of his family or the smallness of his income. They must be particularly on their guard against petitions from the parishes to be provided for, whether on behalf of a curate that has laboured among them, or any other individual. They must examine carefully, and judge as before God, how far any person possesses the qualifications suited to the particular parish, and by that consideration *alone* must they be determined in their appointment of him.[54]

Simeon asked a friend, 'Why have I bought those livings? Not to present a good man to each, but to fill them with men who shall prove great and leading characters in the church of God.'[55] Many of these ministers had been trained and influenced by Simeon at Cambridge. One such recipient of Simeon's patronage was Francis Close who became the incumbent of Cheltenham in 1826. He recalled that the aim of Simeon's life had been 'To promote the glory of God, to further the cause of Christ, at home, abroad, among Jews and heathens, and throughout the world; for this he lived, and in the pursuit of these noble objects he spent no less than fifty-six years of his life. A more conscientious man I never knew.'[56]

Lord Shaftesbury (1801-1885)

John Wolffe

The outward course of Anthony Ashley-Cooper's life was a paradigm of the nineteenth-century British aristocracy.[1] He was born in Grosvenor Square in 1801; one grandfather was an earl, the other a duke; he was educated at Harrow School and Christ Church, Oxford, and elected to parliament at the age of twenty-five on the basis of his family connections. His political instincts were, and remained, profoundly conservative. He married Lady Emily ('Minny') Cowper, the daughter of Countess Cowper and, most probably, of the future prime minister Lord Palmerston.[2] On his father's death in 1851 he inherited an earldom and over twenty thousand acres of central southern England.

In other respects, however, Shaftesbury's career and outlook challenged narrow aristocratic stereotypes. Able and well-connected though he was, from his mid-thirties onwards he neither sought nor held government office. Rather his political energies were devoted to the welfare of those less fortunate than himself, notably in securing legislation to control conditions and hours of work in factories and mines and in measures to regulate the treatment of the mentally ill. Above all his fervent and committed Christianity contrasted with the conventional religiosity of his class, and was the spiritual and ideological mainspring of his life and actions.

In contrast to many of the figures discussed in this book Shaftesbury's Christian faith found expression in political and philanthropic action rather than in preaching and publication. His 'heart of faith' is, however, copiously but somewhat treacherously documented by his extensive diaries, kept intermittently from 1825 and systematically for nearly fifty years from the later 1830s until his last illness took hold in 1885. They were (unlike some diaries kept by public figures) never intended for publication and contained intense and spontaneous outpourings, revealing heartfelt Christian convictions, but also agonizing self-doubt, self-pity and hypochondria. There were also hasty judgements of situations and individuals. While close attention to the diaries is essential in understanding Shaftesbury's inner life, they also need to be used cautiously. In particular, while they do appear to have been a safety valve releasing a darker, even disturbed, side of his nature, they need to be set against the evidence that his public persona was always a tightly controlled, courteous and positive one.

Shaftesbury's Christian convictions developed gradually between his childhood and his mid-thirties. His early spiritual formation owed nothing to his parents, but a lot to a family servant, Maria Milles, who was probably an Anglican evangelical or Methodist convert. She told him Bible stories and taught him to pray his first prayers, words which he continued to repeat throughout his life. By the time she died when the boy was ten she had trained him in a habit of regular prayer and Bible reading.[3] During his teenage years, which he was later to characterize as a period of 'idleness', such spiritual discipline appears to have receded, but he still retained 'Christian instincts'.[4] After graduating from Oxford in 1822, Shaftesbury followed aristocratic convention by taking a Grand Tour of Europe, and in Vienna in late 1824 or early 1825 fell desperately in love with Antoinette van Leykan, the daughter of a diplomat married to an Italian singer, whose musical and theatrical connections were perceived as disreputable in good society. The details of the affair are now unknown, but it ended with Shaftesbury returning disconsolate to England, acknowledging that he had loved 'furiously' and 'imprudently', but that Providence had intervened to save him from an attachment to an 'angel' with 'a halo of hell'. The incident, however, 'commenced a course of self-knowledge for me', and it appears no coincidence that from 1825 onwards he began to keep a diary and to show greater interest in Christianity. Thus he recorded reading a discourse by the leading Scottish evangelical Thomas Chalmers, and in October avowed that he had 'a great mind to found a policy upon the Bible'. In 1826 he read another key evangelical text, Thomas Scott's Bible commentary, and on his twenty-fifth birthday that April 1826 he was able to look back with resignation on his encounter with Antoinette, and to perceive that God had an as yet unrevealed purpose for his own life.[5]

During the next few years there was growing evidence of deep-seated Christian commitment. He became a serious student of the Scriptures: for example on a Sunday in 1829 he read the whole of Revelation at a sitting, observing that this made 'the general scope more easy of comprehension'. He even aspired to learn Hebrew (with a first class degree in Classics he already had excellent Greek) in order to be able to read the whole Bible in the original languages. He believed that the 'precepts and wisdom of the Bible' provided the best possible foundation for other intellectual activity. He also loved silent prayer 'in solitude and contemplation'.[6] Meanwhile Shaftesbury was seeking a Christian wife, a desire that was fulfilled when he married Minny in June 1830. At first sight her Whiggish family connections and lack of overt godliness made her an unlikely choice for the earnest pious Tory politician, but she clearly possessed or rapidly acquired Christian convictions that, albeit less intense than his own, enabled her to be the soulmate he craved. The marriage was to be a very happy one, with a sense of genuine partnership and shared interests.

The question of whether Shaftesbury had always been an evangelical, or whether rather he became one in his thirties is not easy to resolve. In fact his spiritual development illustrates how the boundaries of earlier nineteenth-century evangelicalism were somewhat permeable. The inspiration of the lives and writings of Hannah More and William Wilberforce had attracted significant but qualified support among the elite. In the 1830s, however, partly due to its own theological development, partly in response to political crisis, and partly in reaction to the Oxford Movement, the dominant mood of Anglican evangelicalism became more dogmatic and partisan. Shaftesbury's own religious development needs to be understood against this background. His biographer perceived a 'growing intensity' in his religious life in the early 1830s and in June 1834 he had written in his diary that he now had 'a deeper sense' of religion than when he left Oxford over a decade before.[7] By the late 1830s he became very publicly associated with the evangelical party in the Church of England, above all through his chairmanship of the Church Pastoral Aid Society (CPAS) from its formation in 1836. Judgements, however, have differed as to when exactly Shaftesbury's evangelicalism became clear-cut, especially as no datable conversion experience is recorded. A case can be made for the later 1820s in view of his growing reverence for the Bible, and increasingly conspicuous piety: as early as April 1829 he was being regarded as a 'Saint', contemporary slang for an evangelical. On the other hand, there is no evidence that at this time he subscribed to characteristic evangelical beliefs on original sin and the atonement, which he only began to articulate a few years later.[8]

Shaftesbury's mature faith was intensely Christocentric, suffused with a sense of the reality of the atonement and the prospect of the Second Advent. Some of his most revealing statements of his personal belief were made at deathbeds and times of bereavement, in attributing to those he loved the essence of his own convictions. In 1849 he counselled his dying second son Francis to 'think of nothing but Jesus Christ and Him crucified', and as the boy's epitaph he wrote: 'he only sought forgiveness in the free love and mercy of God through the atonement of a crucified Saviour'. At Lord Palmerston's deathbed in 1865 Shaftesbury 'spoke of sin, of forgiveness, and of sin being washed away only by the blood of our crucified Saviour'. Although devastated when his wife died in 1872, he derived comfort from the recollection that 'She was a sincere, sunny and gentle follower of our Lord; and almost the last words that fell from her lips were "None but Christ"'.[9]

During Shaftesbury's middle and later life, his two closest spiritual confidantes, apart from his wife and his diary, were Edward Bickersteth (1785-1850), a leading evangelical clergyman and popular devotional writer, and Alexander Haldane (1800-1882), a lawyer and the dominant force behind *The Record*, the main Anglican evangelical newspaper. The development of his friendship with Bickersteth in the mid-1830s appears to have been instrumental in the reinforcing of his evangelical convictions, and in particular to his development of premillennial beliefs regarding the Second Advent. While for some premillennialism can lead to fatalism and a sense of the futility of human action, for Shaftesbury, as indeed for Bickersteth, it had the reverse effect in galvanizing vigorous activism in the belief that he must not be found negligent when the Master returned. Moreover for Shaftesbury, Jesus's return was not something to be feared, but to be anticipated with joyful expectation. After Bickersteth's death Shaftesbury recalled him not as a prophet of doom, but for his 'warmth' and 'joy in good'.[10] His friendship with Haldane developed in the late 1840s, and their relations were marked by 'intimacy' from around the early 1860s. His summary of the qualities he most valued in Haldane, written when the latter died in 1882, may also be taken as an expression of his own convictions and manner of life:

> He believed intensely in the Lord Jesus, His power, His office, His work. He intensely loved Him, and ever talked with a holy relish and full desire for the Second Advent. A long life . . .[11] was devoted to the advancement of Christ's Kingdom and to the temporal and eternal welfare of the human race. His sole hope was in the all-atoning blood of our blessed Saviour; any approach to a doctrine of works was his abhorrence. . . .[12]

Haldane has been credited with influencing Shaftesbury towards a more 'harsh and strident' evangelicalism in his later years, and his views certainly appeared more entrenched as he aged. Here too, however, Shaftesbury's position needs to be set against wider changes in the religious climate which meant that attitudes that seemed very much in the evangelical mainstream in the 1840s were beginning to look old-fashioned by the 1870s. Paradoxically, although he came to be perceived as the lay leader of Anglican evangelicalism in the half century between Wilberforce's death in 1833 and his own in 1885, Shaftesbury always resisted unequivocal church party identification. In 1845, for example, he observed that his language was 'not half fiery enough' for the zealots of Exeter Hall (their main meeting place in the Strand) and confided to his diary, 'What a blessing to me it is that I am [not] held by the strings of a party either indoors [that is, in parliament] or out!'[13]

It is noteworthy that Shaftesbury had already committed himself in 1833 to the cause of factory reform, his best-known political concern, before his evangelical religious convictions were fully developed. Indeed rather uncharacteristically and in contrast to Wilberforce's long-considered commitment to the cause of slave trade abolition, he initially took up the issue without much prior thought in response to an urgent request to replace the movement's previous parliamentary spokesman, Michael Sadler, who had lost his seat in the general election of 1832.[14] While he recalled praying and meditating before giving an affirmative answer, his motivation then derived from Tory paternalism and general Christian benevolence, rather than from any specifically evangelical ideology. As time went on spiritual motives came more to the fore in driving his social concern, as was well demonstrated in the peroration to one of his greatest parliamentary speeches, when in 1843 he moved for the government to give serious consideration to measures for providing moral and religious education for the working classes:

> We owe to the poor of our land a weighty debt. We call them improvident and immoral, and many of them are so; but that improvidence and that immorality are the results, in a great measure of our neglect, and, in not a little, of our example. . . . Only let us declare this night, that we will enter on a novel and better course – that we will seek their temporal through their eternal welfare – and the half of our work will then have been achieved. There are many hearts to be won, many minds to be instructed, and many souls to be saved. . . . [15]

In the meantime Shaftesbury's extra-parliamentary activities, notably the CPAS and his encouragement in the 1850s of special services for the working class in Exeter Hall and London theatres, demonstrated his commitment to directly evangelistic work.

Shaftesbury was a passionately loyal son of the Church of England, and his evangelicalism cannot be separated from his Anglicanism. That loyalty was in part a product of his class and upbringing in the 'high-and-dry' school which, he later recalled, meant that as a child he believed the Bible Society to be 'an evil and revolutionary institution'. He had also considered it 'a meritorious thing to hate Dissenters'.[16] The latter prejudice, at least, proved difficult entirely to shake off. It was to some extent reawakened in 1843 when nonconformist opposition prevented the government proceeding with his cherished plans for the education of factory children. They had objected to the scheme as unduly favourable to the Church of England while he, in the aftermath of this disappointment, set his face against 'combined education', affirming that the Church must have 'our own schools, our Catechism, our Liturgy, our Articles, our Homilies, our faith, our own teaching of God's Word.'[17] In the mid-1840s, Shaftesbury remained very concerned about the vulnerability of the Church to nonconformist political attacks. A more positive attitude was, however, apparent in his view of the Evangelical Alliance, founded in 1846, and bringing together Protestant Christians of a wide range of denominations from both sides of the Atlantic. Although sceptical as to the movement's capacity to have a significant practical impact, he was still pleased to see that 'a thousand people of various forms of Christian belief, of jarring sects . . . assembled together day after day; joined in fervent prayer; mutually confessed their errors, and sins towards each other' and affirmed the 'leading principles of revealed Religion'.[18] Moreover, when he perceived cooperation with nonconformists as furthering the cause of the gospel he was delighted to support it – in November 1845, after visiting a Ragged School, he wrote, 'Many Dissenters, but it is high time to be thinking where we agree, not where we differ.' He was also a longstanding and prominent supporter of interdenominational organizations, notably the London City Mission and the YMCA. In his later years, in the light of his perception that attacks on Christianity itself were increasing, his attitude to nonconformists mellowed further. This attitude was evident, for example, in his readiness in 1881 to lay the memorial stone at a Baptist Chapel, writing that 'Externals must now be secondary in consideration.'[19]

Shaftesbury's major opportunity to shape the Church of England came in 1855 when Palmerston became Prime Minister, and turned to his step-son-in-law as a key advisor in ecclesiastical matters. Initially the subsequent episcopal appointments showed a preponderance of evangelicals, but no more than were necessary to redress their previous under-representation on the bench. A particular concern was to appoint men who would conciliate nonconformists rather than confront them. During the later years of Palmerston's administration, which continued with a short break until 1865, the strategy was rather to maintain a balance between church parties while avoiding extremes. The fear of Shaftesbury's critics that he would persuade Palmerston to advance more militant evangelicals proved unjustified.[20]

Shaftesbury's attitudes to the two most prominent religious minorities in Victorian Britain – Roman Catholics and Jews – were an important aspect of his own outlook. Initially he lacked animosity to Roman Catholics. His early love, Antoinette van Leykan, was a Roman Catholic. In 1829 he supported the removal of Roman Catholic civil disabilities in the belief that no safeguards for liberty could be effective, except 'the spirit of a nation'. In 1833 he attended High Mass in Milan Cathedral, in the absence of a Protestant place of worship, although he found the ceremony 'tedious and unspiritual'.[21] During the 1830s, however, he became increasingly concerned at the advance of Catholicism in Britain, an attitude which was reinforced by Edward Bickersteth who in early 1836, at the very time Shaftesbury became friendly with him, published a tract entitled *The Progress of Popery*. Bickersteth denounced the system of popery – which he distinguished from individual professing Roman Catholics – especially on the grounds that it upheld human works rather than justification by faith, and that it was condemned in the prophetic writings of Scripture as 'the Mystery of Iniquity, the Man of Sin, the Antichrist, and the Apocalyptic Babylon'.[22] Such convictions appear to have imprinted themselves on Shaftesbury. Subsequent events, notably the enactment in 1845 of permanent government support for the seminary at Maynooth in Ireland, and the restoration in 1850 of the Roman Catholic episcopal hierarchy in England and Wales heightened his anxieties. He viewed the 1848 Revolutions in continental Europe in a strongly eschatological framework, believing them to represent divine judgement on popery.[23] He took a prominent part in the Protestant movements of the early 1850s, the Protestant Defence Committee and the Protestant Alliance. Nevertheless, following Bickersteth, he was careful that his passionate opposition to an impersonal 'popery' did not translate into personal attacks on Roman Catholics. In May 1849 he expressed strong reservations about the 'violent, vituperative and declamatory' language of the resolutions to be put to a public meeting of the recently-formed Irish Church Missions to Roman Catholics and was relieved when his son's serious illness gave him an excuse to withdraw from the chair.[24] In March 1851, speaking in the House of Commons on proposed legislation against the new Roman Catholic bishops, he avoided 'violent' language, was careful to distinguish between the priesthood and the laity, and affirmed the loyalty of English Roman Catholics.[25]

Indeed in the wake of the Tractarian Oxford Movement Shaftesbury was, if anything, more deeply concerned by the growth of Anglo-Catholicism within the Church of England than by Roman Catholicism outside it. In April 1850 he wrote that 'The pretexts of the Tractarian party are in the highest degree, Roman, Popish and autocratical'.[26] Roman Catholics were at least open opponents whereas Tractarians were subverting Protestantism from inside. In a memorable analogy he described popery in 1851 as 'spiritual fornication', but 'Puseyism' as 'spiritual adultery'.[27] His hatred and fear of the Tractarians was later reflected in his advice to Palmerston on patronage: while Shaftesbury was willing to countenance the appointment of the Broad Churchman Archibald Campbell Tait as Bishop of London in 1856, and even the appointment of moderate High Church bishops such as Charles Ellicott and Edward Browne, he consistently warned Palmerston off men who showed 'any approximation to Popery'.[28] In the 1860s and 1870s he strenuously opposed ritualism. In 1851 he had publicly stated that his loyalty to the Church of England was not unconditional: it must 'continue to be scriptural' and if it failed to do so he was prepared to leave it.[29] The vigour of his hostility to Anglo-Catholicism, and to a lesser extent to liberal Anglicanism, stemmed from his anxiety to ensure that he would never in the event feel himself obliged to take such a painful step.

Shaftesbury's conviction that the British parliament should remain exclusively Christian led him to oppose the admission of Jews until in 1858 he decided that further objection would be fruitless.[30] In other respects, however, his attitude to Jews contrasted markedly with his attitude to Catholics, a difference that was rooted in his eschatological beliefs. Whereas he believed 'popery' to be condemned in Scripture and subject to destruction by God in the last times, he believed that the return of the Jews to Palestine and their conversion to Christianity was a necessary preliminary to the Second Coming. Hence he took a leading part in the establishment of a joint Anglican-Lutheran bishopric of Jerusalem in 1841, and was from 1848 President of the London Society for Promoting Christianity amongst the Jews. Nor was his sympathy for the Jews merely a matter of seeking their conversion to Christianity: in the 1850s he urged the government to use its influence with the Turkish government, whom Britain was supporting against Russia in the Crimean War, to persuade them to set up a Jewish homeland. Even in his eighties he showed impressive energy in efforts to ameliorate the situation of Jews escaping Russian persecution.[31]

Shaftesbury's interest in a Jewish homeland was a key strand in a wider global Christian vision. As a young man he had held junior ministerial office as a member of the India Board of Control, and he continued to take a close interest in the affairs of the sub-continent, over which he believed Britain had been given a 'sublime guardianship'.[32] In 1843-4 he strongly criticized the injustice of government action in the dispossession and imprisonment of a family of local rulers, the Ameers of Scinde. In response to the 'Mutiny' of 1857 he balanced an insistence on meting out retribution to the 'rebels' with the advocacy of schemes to secure the spiritual, moral and material betterment of India. He also took a strong interest in the religious and political condition of continental Europe, for example in relation to the unification of Italy, and the United States. After the publication in 1852 of Harriet Beecher Stowe's *Uncle Tom's Cabin*, he sought to mobilize British opinion against slavery and gave strong public support to the North in the American Civil War.[33]

Shaftesbury died peacefully on a sunny autumn afternoon in 1885.[34] Although eighty-four he had been publicly active almost to the last, but was nevertheless prepared for an event that had no terrors for him. He was buried in the little village church near his ancestral home at Wimborne St Giles in Dorset, with a memorial tablet that, on his own instructions, carried no eulogy, but only his name, dates of birth and death, and three biblical texts he had chosen himself: 'What hast thou that thou didst not receive?' (1 Corinthians 4:7), 'Let him that thinketh he standeth take heed lest he fall' (1 Corinthians 10:12) and the last verse in the Bible, 'Surely I come quickly. Amen. Even so, come Lord Jesus' (Revelation 22:20). They well sum up central features of his Christian faith: his insistence on the primacy of the words of Scripture; his sense of absolute dependence on God; his consciousness of responsibility as a steward of divine gifts to humanity; his awareness of the pervasiveness of sin and failure; and his assured sense of relationship with Jesus Christ, whose return in glory would be an imminent reality.[35]

J.C. Ryle (1816-1900)

David Bebbington

John Charles Ryle, first Bishop of Liverpool from 1880 to 1900, had a striking physical presence.[1] Standing six feet three and a half inches tall, he wore a flowing beard that gave him the appearance of an Old Testament prophet. The *Liverpool Daily Post*, in an editorial on his eightieth birthday in 1896, expressed a widespread view of the bishop. 'Erect, stalwart, hearty and cordial', declared the newspaper, 'he is the model of what a venerable prelate ought to be.'[2] Ryle was a man hard to forget. But what were his convictions and achievements? This chapter attempts to evaluate his outlook and role as one of the most eminent of Victorian churchmen.

Ryle was born in 1816 into a prosperous household at Macclesfield in Cheshire, but in 1841, a few years after he came down from Oxford, the family banking firm collapsed. The shame of bankruptcy and relative poverty accentuated the young man's deep-seated personal shyness. The loss of his first wife within three years of marriage and the permanent invalidity of his second further reinforced Ryle's tendency to withdrawal. He served in country parishes, Helmingham (from 1844) and then Stradbroke (from 1861) in Suffolk, and so was able to spend a good deal of time in writing. The work for which he was famous in the earlier part of his career was the series of *Expository Thoughts on the Gospels* (1856-73), designed for reading aloud at family prayers or when visiting the sick. He also turned many of his sermons into tracts with snappy titles such as *Do you want a friend?* and *Are you an heir?*, selling as many as twelve million copies during his lifetime. His other main body of writing was on the puritans of seventeenth-century Suffolk. His lucid style, formed by the discipline of preaching to rustic audiences, made him an unusually accessible writer. Until his appointment by a Conservative government to the new see of Liverpool, Ryle was best known for his literary output.

Ryle was celebrated as a writer of the evangelical school. Evangelicals so stressed the place of the Bible in religion that others sometimes accused them of bibliolatry. In 1891 Ryle produced a reply to that charge, adding side-thrusts against other parties: 'Let us not fear being idolaters of this blessed book. Men may easily make an idol of the church, of ministers, of sacraments, or of intellect. Men cannot make an idol of the Word.'[3] There was equal commitment to the cross. The central evangelical doctrine was the atonement, the sacrificial death of Christ, and in 1852 Ryle published a tract called *The Cross*. Without the event of Calvary, he argued, religion is like 'a compass without a needle'.[4] Like other evangelicals, Ryle made conversion a further favourite theme, urging the experience on his readers. For Ryle personally, conversion took place in 1837, while he was at Oxford. He had been seriously concerned about religion for some time, but then in church he heard a lesson read from Ephesians chapter 2 with pauses between phrases: 'By grace are ye saved – through faith – and that not of yourselves – it is the gift of God.'[5] Taking these words to heart, he consciously accepted the grace and so passed through conversion. A fourth consistent dimension of evangelicalism upheld by Ryle was its dedication to activism. In his first five years as a bishop, for instance, he preached in as many as 150 of the 187 churches in his diocese.[6] His clergy praised him on his eightieth birthday for 'his unceasing activity day and night'.[7] Ryle was as much an exponent of activism as he was of the other three core qualities of evangelicals.

Ryle is particularly known for his teaching on holiness, and so that theme calls for more extended treatment. The theological framework of his convictions in this area was Calvinism. By no means all evangelical Anglicans of the time professed the reformed faith in its totality, but Ryle did. He emphasised God's initiative in redemption, holding that some were predestined to salvation. At the 1868 general election, he published a tract called *Your Election*, arguing that God had chosen those sinners who would be saved. Ryle was not, like John Wesley, an Arminian, believing that all could be saved since each was free to respond to the gospel. His theological heroes, rather, were seventeenth-century puritans. In his book on *Holiness*, the theologians quoted are Richard Sibbes, Thomas Manton and John Owen, together with Samuel Rutherford, the seventeenth-century Scottish Presbyterian, and William Romaine, the eighteenth-century Anglican evangelical. Yet Ryle did not embrace puritan divinity without reservations. He offered two qualifications about its shortcomings. In the first place, it was unnecessarily complicated by elaborate metaphysics. Ryle denounced the 'long, supra-scriptural, systematic statements of theology' which darkened the pages of the puritans.[8] Instead he favoured simplicity.

In the second place, he considered some of the puritans fell into the trap of encouraging undue introspection over sins. Ryle repudiated 'extravagant language about repentance'.[9] He thought that believers, like hypochondriacs, could become too preoccupied with their own spiritual ailments. They would then give little time to work for God. So in theology Ryle was a Calvinist, owing a heavy debt to the puritans, but a moderate one, retaining an independent judgement.

Much of Ryle's teaching about holiness was hammered out in opposition to the views of the Oxford Movement. He accepted its view that effort was needed in the spiritual life. The difficulty he saw in the Tractarian position lay elsewhere. John Henry Newman, Edward Pusey and their disciples failed to make a sharp distinction fundamental in puritan thought, the contrast between justification and sanctification. For Newman, the two were much the same, because faith and obedience constituted an identical disposition. For puritans, however, justification was God's gift of regenerating grace, which made a person a Christian. It was given to faith, not obedience. Sanctification, on the other hand, was God's gift of grace that engrafted holiness into the life of a person who was already a Christian. It was given while a believer put effort into good works. Ryle wholly concurred with the distinction between justification and sanctification, holding it to be crucial. If the two were confused, then justification might seem to be conferred as a reward for good works. Ryle insisted that individuals must first come to Christ in faith and only afterwards seek to advance in sanctification. For holiness there was a precondition of personal faith.

Likewise Ryle was hostile to the teaching of the Keswick Convention about holiness. The convention, which was launched in 1875, taught not merely that justification was by faith alone, but also that sanctification came to the believer in exactly the same way. The Christian, on this view, became holy not by good works, but by personal trust. In *Holiness* (1877), however, Ryle attacked the Keswick idea that the believer moves into a state of holiness at a particular point of crisis. Rather, holiness is the result of a sustained conflict against sin. Ryle criticised the notion that there were three types of people: sinners, penitents seeking a higher spiritual life and saints who had attained it. There were, on the contrary, only two classes: unbelievers and believers. And Ryle rejected the fundamental Keswick notion that a person may reach holiness by trusting and no more. Holiness by faith, according to Ryle, is not a New Testament idea. Sanctification comes, according to Ryle, by '*practical exertion*'.[10] It is true that Ryle soon accepted that the Keswick movement could do good. By 1879 he had mellowed sufficiently to preach in the Lake District town immediately before the convention and in 1892 he offered prayer within the convention itself. Yet he did not change his mind. For anybody to attain holiness, more than mere faith was required. So Ryle's conception of holiness, firmly grounded in puritan theology, was equally dismissive of the Oxford and Keswick movements.

Ryle was also remarkable for his views on the mission of the church, views which, as bishop, he was able to translate into practice. His priority was securing able clergy. Their work, he believed, was many-sided, but two elements were the priorities. One was pastoral ministry. It was possible, he remarked in one of his triennial charges as bishop, for a minister to give too much attention to public work and too little to regular pastoral activity.[11] The other primary element was preaching. 'A minister's sermons', he wrote in 1856, 'should be incomparably the first and chief thing in his thoughts every week that he lives.'[12] The visiting and preaching of the clergy were the cutting edge of mission. Nevertheless the laity played a prominent part in Ryle's strategy. He wanted ordinary churchgoers to be able to give a reason for the hope that was within them. In an early tract on the death of Georgina Tollemache, the wife of the landed proprietor at Helmingham, Ryle praised her for 'always trying to win individual souls for Jesus Christ'.[13] Yet Ryle was no fanatic, for in a later tract he commented that in personal testimony 'we need common sense and discretion, as well as faithfulness and zeal'.[14] Laypeople could take up the role of Scripture Readers or Bible Women, people employed to go from door to door to read and sell the Bible among the working classes. After ten years in his diocese, Ryle could boast about fifty licensed Scripture Readers and thirty Bible Women.[15] In his day, however, there had to be special attention to people of influence. Ryle regretted that Liverpool, because it was so urbanised, lacked many nobility or large landed proprietors.[16] He therefore concentrated, though with mixed success, on galvanising the middle classes, especially the merchants and industrialists. He urged the heads of great concerns in the manufacturing and colliery districts to have face-to-face relations with their employees so that they could influence them for good.[17] Ryle's aim was to mobilise the whole church, ordained and lay, for more effective propagation of the faith.

Ryle believed in supplementing regular church work with special missions. In 1870 he argued that the Church of England should establish a body of evangelists who could be sent into parishes under the authority of the bishop to preach for two to four weeks even if the local clergyman did not want them. 'The Church of England,' he declared, 'has made an idol of her parochial system.'[18] This was in some measure to anticipate the idea of Wilson Carlile, who in 1882 established the Church Army – though subsequently Ryle did not think highly of the Church Army since it cost too much.[19] As bishop, he supported efforts of a more *ad hoc* kind. He appointed evangelists, two for Walton, one for Bootle.[20] He supported the American revivalists Moody and Sankey when they visited Liverpool in 1883 and the Anglican evangelist Hay Aitken when he held a city-wide mission in 1894, though, according to the press, the latter stressed 'the utter undesirableness of excitement'. 'This', went on the newspaper, 'is the true note of the Church of England.'[21] In addition Ryle gave active encouragement to missions to particular groups: to Jews, prostitutes, soldiers and sailors.[22] Clearly he was not restricted in the methods he used and fostered. He was willing to be flexible in his aim of winning people to Christian discipleship.

Part of the mission of the church was the provision of buildings. Ryle was confronted on his arrival in Liverpool with low church attendance rates. In 1881 only ten per cent of the population of the city attended the Church of England.[23] Part of the explanation, the bishop concluded, was the distribution of church buildings. Several churches had been left largely empty in areas that had been turned into dockland while some other parts of the city were inadequately provided with buildings. Kirkdale, for example, contained two parishes where in each the number of inhabitants was over 20,000.[24] Nowhere outside London was the population denser. Ryle's response was to break up the people into small districts of 5,000, later 3,500, each with a building for worship. During his episcopate, 44 new churches were consecrated, though the pace slowed in the 1890s. There was even more emphasis on new mission rooms, licensed for non-liturgical worship, of which 85 were started in Ryle's time.[25] This fresh provision went a considerable way towards supplying church accommodation for the people of the diocese. In one aspect of building, however, Ryle was unsuccessful, for no cathedral was begun in his lifetime. This failure was not the result of any lack of interest on the bishop's part, at least at first, but was because of interminable disputes over the rival claims of potential sites. With that notable exception, he pushed through a vigorous campaign to provide church buildings.

A further dimension of Ryle's blueprint for mission consisted of his schemes for church reform. He is sometimes represented as a fossilised figure, a throwback to a bygone age, but that judgement does not do justice to the broad programme of reform he advocated in 1870. He argued for more bishops, smaller dioceses. Ryle actually recommended that Lancashire should have three or four dioceses,[26] which was perhaps a reason why, ten years later, his name was thought suitable for the new diocese of Liverpool in that county. The appeal for more bishops was his most popular proposal, but there were many others. Bishops, he contended, should not automatically sit in the House of Lords, but might elect four or five of their number to represent them there. Again, he argued for a bishop's council, partly consisting of laity, so that the diocese would become less dependent on one individual. Ryle was of the opinion that a council would deliver dioceses from 'bold and brash Bishops' who did too much and from 'timid and cautious Bishops' who did nothing.[27] After he arrived in Liverpool, however, Ryle set up no advisory body of this kind. In 1870 he also believed that deans should be abolished. Bishops should supervise their own cathedrals, living in the dean's house. Again, however, there was no sign of this policy being adopted in Liverpool, where Ryle took little interest in the worship of the parish church that was used as a temporary cathedral.[28] Likewise he altered his views about diocesan conferences, annual gatherings of the clergy. In 1868 he opposed them, but after several subsequent modifications of his standpoint he set up, as bishop, an annual conference for the clergy of Liverpool.[29] In all these policies, with their alterations, his reasoning was strikingly pragmatic. There was a remarkable absence of stiff intransigence from his approach.

Although Ryle placed public work below pastoral care on the clerical agenda, he showed a significant degree of involvement in the wider community. Like most Victorian clergy, he paid attention to education. At Stradbroke he erected a parish school. In Liverpool he championed the Church of England schools, raising money on their behalf. Equally naturally, he played a prominent part in local charities. Thus he regularly supported Mrs Birt's Sheltering Home, an orphanage that sent destitute children to Canada.[30] Beyond that, he showed zeal for the defence of Sunday rest during his whole ministry. At Liverpool, as in many other cities, there was a prolonged debate over the Sunday opening of museums. Ryle resisted firmly, helping in 1884 to prevent the council from deciding to open them but by 1891 losing the struggle.[31] He also took up the temperance cause. Ryle was never a total abstainer, but he spoke of drunkenness as 'the most dreadful of any of the sins by which England was disgraced'.[32] He urged his clergy to preach an annual temperance sermon and supported the Church of England Temperance Society. Ryle, however, did not venture into the social gospel adopted by many evangelical nonconformists during his episcopate. He refused to be drawn into industrial disputes with a view to mediation and firmly denounced 'the wave of unhealthy Socialism' in 1895.[33] For Ryle, community involvement had its limits. But he was not inflexible in mission, as he showed over church reform; and his public work revealed that he was by no means narrow either.

A further dimension of Ryle's life and thought was concerned with relations within and between churches. He was ever a loyal churchman, spending a good deal of time urging his fellow evangelicals not to leave the Church of England. 'Secession', he wrote in 1892, 'is not necessary.'[34] Ryle's *Knots Untied* (1874) is an attempt to show the members of his own party that their qualms about the Church of England could all be overcome. Evangelicals, Ryle insisted, were the truest churchmen, despite all the claims of High Churchmen, because they were of one mind with the Protestant reformers: Ridley, Hooper, Latimer and specially Cranmer, the chief architect of the *Book of Common Prayer*. Ryle's churchmanship was exemplified in his defence of the establishment. He was thoroughly dismayed when, in 1868, W.E. Gladstone as Liberal leader announced his intention of introducing Irish disestablishment. The Protestant church was being thrown off by the state in a land where it needed all the support it could gather against the hostility of the Roman Catholic majority. Ryle steeled himself to resist a similar measure for England. In 1885 he issued a prayer for use during the sitting of parliament in favour of the 'Scriptural National Church'.[35] He was passionately committed to the Church of England as established.

Ryle, who in his youth had been a captain in the Cheshire Yeomanry, was very much an ecclesiastical combatant. A great deal of his effort was directed against the Roman Catholic Church because, he believed, it gave false guidance about the kernel of the faith. When people wanted to know the path to peace with God, the priest stood in the way. Ryle called in 1868 for a 'bold and outspoken *Protestantism*'.[36] He was a keen supporter of Irish Church Missions, an Anglican organisation for the quixotic project of turning all the people of Ireland into Protestants, and visited Dublin twice during the 1860s in support of this body.[37] To Ryle the Roman Catholic Church was not an ecumenical partner but a dangerous rival. More of his attention, however, in the later part of his career focused on the ritualists, clergy within the Church of England who were adopting elaborate ceremonial for worship that appeared to be an imitation of Roman Catholic practice. This body of men, according to Ryle in 1881, was 'determined to unprotestantize the Church of England'.[38] He objected to anything that seemed to symbolise an unreformed church. Thus at his consecration in York Minster he refused to wear a cope and mitre.[39] Because of his fervour in the anti-ritualist cause, it was natural for Ryle to join the Church Association, founded in 1865 to support legal challenges to doubtful liturgical innovations. He became a vice-president from 1870 to 1880 and was widely regarded as a leading opponent of ritualism.

On his elevation to the bench, Ryle was faced with a knot that was impossible to untie. He resigned from the Church Association because it might seem improper for a bishop to belong to so partisan a body, knowing in his head that he had to be above party strife; yet in his heart he still concurred in the Association's stance. At St Margaret's, Toxteth Park, the vicar, James Bell Cox, was a prominent ritualist. In 1885 a member of the Liverpool branch of the Church Association formally complained about the liturgical behaviour of Bell Cox on eleven counts. The vicar, for example, was said to have 'knelt and prostrated himself' before the consecrated bread and wine.[40] Bell Cox refused to stop what were technically illegal acts. Most bishops had decided by this point that they would veto ritual prosecutions for the sake of the peace of the church, but Ryle felt that would have been inconsistent with his principles. Consequently Bell Cox was prosecuted in the Chancery Court at York. The court required him to desist; the vicar refused; and so he was sent to Walton Gaol for contempt of court. He was soon released on a technicality, but his imprisonment gained him fame and public sympathy. The legal case dragged on until 1892, when the prosecutor gave up. It was a victory for Bell Cox and ritualism. Ryle lost in two ways. Among the general public, he was condemned for permitting an acrimonious prosecution. Among many evangelicals, his erstwhile colleagues, he was censured for not backing the prosecution more firmly. It was the least happy aspect of Ryle's episcopate.

Yet Ryle was not solely or even mainly a divisive figure. Alongside his combatant side was a more irenical strain. He took pains, for instance, to try to achieve evangelical unity. The evangelicals, threatened by the growing audacity of the ritualists, were divided about how to respond. Should they resist with all their might, invoking the aid of the law? Or should they concentrate on nothing but religious labours, eschewing legal entanglements? While acknowledging the importance of directly spiritual measures, Ryle tried to rouse his party to organised resistance in a speech subsequently published as *We must Unite!* Within his own church party, Ryle tried to bring men of different opinions together. He also showed a conciliatory spirit towards nonconformists. 'Between us and orthodox Protestant Dissent', he wrote, 'there is but a thin partition wall.'[41] He was friendly with the Baptist minister at Stradbroke and with the Wesleyan Charles Garrett at Liverpool.[42] In accordance with these views, when on holiday at Pitlochry in Scotland, he attended Presbyterian worship.[43] To many it seemed scandalous that a bishop of the Church of England should fraternise to that extent with a non-episcopal church. But Ryle even had a good word for the Unitarians, who were influential in Liverpool. When a High Churchman criticised them, Ryle declared that while Unitarians erred, they did not, as the critic claimed, despise and reject Christ.[44] While it is true that he did not like nonconformists being militant disestablishers, he was sympathetic to nonconformists in themselves.

Within the Church of England Ryle was a pioneer of rapprochement between evangelicals and the main body of High Churchmen. Ritualists remained for him outside the pale, but the majority of the heirs of the Oxford Movement were in a distinct position. They differed only marginally from churchly-minded evangelicals. At the Church Congress of 1878 Ryle urged 'the great duty of cultivating brotherly kindness and avoiding quarrels'.[45] Going to a Church Congress, an annual forum dominated by High Churchmen, was itself a bold step for Ryle. He attended for the first time in 1865, travelled to it again in 1868 and then went regularly from 1870. He was denounced by fellow evangelicals for becoming entangled in a snare, but he persisted. He found it valuable to see and hear High Churchmen, and to be seen and heard himself. 'If I once see a man face to face', he remarked, 'I find it hard to hate him.'[46] Ryle was confident that if evangelicals had dealings with High Churchmen, they would discover that less separated them than they had supposed. His policy as bishop reflected this stance. He preached annually for the High Church missionary agency, the Society for the Propagation of the Gospel, as well as for its evangelical equivalent, the Church Missionary Society.[47] As bishop, he declared in his first charge, he aimed to be 'just and fair and kind' to clergy of every school of thought, whether High, Low, Broad or none of these.[48] Such a guiding principle was no doubt essential in a bishop, but it also sprang from Ryle's inner convictions. He wanted unity in the new diocese of Liverpool. There can be no doubt that this old soldier was a combative churchman, but at the same time he was also a persistent reconciler.

How then should we evaluate this 'venerable prelate'? As a man, John Charles Ryle combined a disabling shyness with notable leadership qualities. As an evangelical, he reflected the emphases on Bible, cross, conversion and activism. In his teaching on holiness, he stoutly resisted the Oxford and Keswick movements, urging disciplined effort in every-day life. His strategy of mission held that the work of the ordained ministry should be backed up by lay support and special missions. He also recognised, in a very practical way, the need for buildings, church reform and public work. On questions of church relations, Ryle was a confirmed churchman, opposed to Rome and ritualism but in favour of bringing Christians towards fuller understanding of each other. At Liverpool this many-sided man contrived to put his convictions into practice, failing only in the difficult choice of a site for a new cathedral and in the impossible task of containing ritualism. But he belonged to more than a single diocese, for his books and tracts exerted a widespread influence over his own and subsequent generations. Bishop Chavasse, Ryle's successor in the see of Liverpool, recorded that he had himself received letters from correspondents all over the world who, supposing that the bishop was still Ryle, thanked him for the help he had given them in his writings.[49] If Ryle was a dedicated servant of the Church of England, he was also a great Christian of global stature.

Frances Ridley Havergal (1836-1879)

Andrew Atherstone

Frances Ridley Havergal was one of the most popular and productive hymn-writers in mid-Victorian Britain. Although her brief career lasted only two decades, cut short by untimely death, her influence and enduring legacy extended throughout the English-speaking world. Her output was prodigious. Alongside indefatigable letter-writing and numerous evangelistic booklets, she published several collections of poetry and hymnody in a short space of time, notably *The Ministry of Song* (1869), *Under the Surface* (1874), *Loyal Responses* (1878) and, posthumously, *Under His Shadow* (1879). By the early twentieth century, two million copies of her works were in circulation.

Havergal was brought up in the Church of England, the daughter of an Anglican clergyman from Worcestershire, but did not personally experience 'spiritual awakening' until at boarding school in Kensington. She never could date her conversion precisely (sometime in the spring of 1851) though it occurred during a mini-revival amongst the girls at the school, long prayed for by the headmistress, Mrs Teed. Three years later, in July 1854 at the age of seventeen, Havergal was confirmed in Worcester Cathedral by Bishop Henry Pepys, a momentous event in her spiritual life. She described her emotions as she knelt before the bishop:

> My feelings when his hands were placed on my head (and there was solemnity and earnestness in the very touch and manner) I cannot describe, they were too confused; but when the words 'Defend, O Lord, this Thy child with Thy heavenly grace, that she may continue Thine for ever, and daily increase in Thy Holy Spirit more and more, until she come unto Thy everlasting kingdom', were solemnly pronounced, if ever my heart followed a prayer it did then, if ever it thrilled with earnest longing not unmixed with joy, it did at the words 'Thine for ever'.

Immediately after the service, Havergal penned the lines

Oh! 'Thine for ever', what a blessed thing
To be for ever His who died for me!
My Saviour, all my life Thy praise I'll sing,
Nor cease my song throughout eternity.[1]

As observed by her biographer, Janet Grierson, the pattern of Havergal's later life and theological priorities is seen here – profound gratitude for the redeeming death of Christ on the cross; a longing to serve Christ in total dedication, especially through the ministry of song; and a conviction that glorious resurrection life is still to come beyond the grave.[2] Throughout Havergal's poems and letters we find her looking back in gratitude and looking forward in hope, while seeking to serve Christ wholeheartedly in the present. This chapter will explore these three aspects of her thought.

Looking Back in Gratitude: 'The Precious Blood of Jesus'

Havergal's sacred poems and hymns are dominantly Christocentric. There are notable exceptions, such as 'The Triune Presence' (1871) and 'Hymn for Ireland' (1873) with their Trinitarian structure; or 'Fresh Springs' (1870) and 'The Faithful Comforter' (1872) about the pouring out of the Holy Spirit. Yet most focus upon the person and work of Jesus Christ – either addressed to him in adoration, or calling people to respond to him in surrender and service, 'with lip and life'. Often Havergal looks back to the cross of Christ, drawing attention to his redeeming work. For example, 'The Precious Blood of Jesus' (1874) and 'The Opened Fountain' (1878) speak in detail of the key implications of Christ's blood-shedding. Likewise her poem, 'Knowing' (1877), begins:

I know the crimson stain of sin,
Defiling all without, within;
But now rejoicingly I know
That He has washed me white as snow.
I praise Him for the cleansing tide,
Because I know that Jesus died.

Meditating on the question of Simon Peter to Jesus Christ, 'Lord, to whom shall we go?' (John 6:68), Havergal proclaimed:

I bring my sins to Thee,
The sins I cannot count,
That all may cleansèd be
In Thy once opened Fount.
I bring them, Saviour, all to Thee
The burden is too great for me.

She understood the death of Christ on Calvary to be a propitiatory sacrifice. Reflecting on the Old Testament prophecy that 'the Lord hath laid on Him the iniquity of us all' (Isaiah 53:6), she penned the lines:

On Thee the Lord
My mighty sins hath laid;
And against Thee Jehovah's sword
Flashed forth its fiery blade.
The stroke of justice fell on Thee,
That it might never fall on me.

It was Havergal's parents who initially helped her to grasp the importance of this truth as a child. When her mother lay dying, in July 1848, she earnestly exhorted her eleven-year-old daughter from her deathbed: 'You are my youngest little girl, and I feel more anxious about you than the rest. I do pray for the Holy Spirit to lead you and guide you. And remember, nothing but the precious blood of Christ can make you clean and lovely in God's sight.'[3] Havergal exhibited a similar emphasis throughout her life, as she urged others to turn to Christ without delay. In 1877 she wrote to a young friend:

I hear you go back to school on Thursday; are you to go back doubtful, uneasy, fearful, dissatisfied, *alone*? or, is it to be going back *with Jesus*, *safe* in Him, *happy* in Him? When the Holy Spirit stirs up a heart to feel uneasy, it is very solemn, because it is His doing; Satan will do his best to say 'peace, peace, when there is no peace'. It is very solemn, because it results either in grieving that loving Spirit by stifling His secret call, *or* in passing from death unto life: the one or the other, I know of no other alternative. Which shall it be? Don't linger just outside the gate of the city of refuge; *just* outside is danger, perhaps destruction; you are not safe for one instant till you are inside.

She went on to explain that if her young correspondent remained unforgiven then 'there is but a step between you and hell . . . don't dare to sleep another night with condemnation upon you'. If, however, her sins were borne by Jesus then she would be 'free, gloriously free!': 'He only asks you to believe that He has borne them, in His own body, on the tree, and that Jehovah hath laid them *on Him*'.[4]

Havergal was painfully aware in her own life of her need for cleansing by the blood of Christ. In her secret *Autobiography* she reflected upon the state of her inner life:

Never for one moment, even from my earliest childhood, have I ever been tempted to think otherwise of myself than as a great and miserable and helpless sinner. Never have I dared to think myself 'as good as others', for even as a little child I knew and felt the sinfulness of my own heart. Never has the shadow of a hope in my own righteousness, or of any trust in myself, crossed my mind. . . . every year shows me more and more the utter deceitfulness of the heart: 'Who can know it!' Oh the comfort of thinking that there is One who *knows* it, and can therefore cleanse its most hidden chambers from their dark pollution.[5]

She often mourned her lukewarmness in prayer, her wandering thoughts, her lack of love, her selfishness and her pride (led astray by 'the wild intoxication of public applause'[6]). She writes:

I want to make the most of my life, & to do *the best* with it, but here I feel my desires & motives need much purifying. . . . Oh that He would indeed purify me & make me white, at *any* cost![7]

No one professing to be a Christian at all could possible have had a more cloudy, fearing, doubting, sinning, and wandering heart history than mine has been through many years.[8]

Aware of her desperate need, Havergal was resolved to fix her eyes 'upon Christ simply as the Substitute, the Lamb slain'.[9] She longed 'to rest more simply on the Lord Jesus & His finished work'.[10]

After more than a decade of deep, and often despondent, spiritual struggles, Havergal's Christian life took a dramatic turn in Advent 1873. It felt to her as if she had been raised up by the Holy Spirit from the 'sunless ravines' on to the 'highway of holiness'.[11] On several occasions she felt 'literally overwhelmed and overpowered with the realization of God's unspeakable goodness to me.'[12] This blessing came partly through reading a small tract, *All for Jesus!* (1871), and partly through a fresh appreciation of words from 1 John 1:7 – 'the blood of Jesus Christ his Son cleanseth us from all sin' – a text which became so important to her that she had it inscribed on her tomb. Havergal came to understand this cleansing as a present experience, not just a past event:

It was that one word 'cleanseth' which opened the door of a very glory of hope and joy to me. I had never seen the force of the tense before, a continual present, always a present tense, not a present which the next moment becomes a past. It *goes on* cleansing, and I have no words to tell how my heart rejoices in it. Not a coming to be cleansed in the fountain only, but a *remaining* in the fountain, so that it may and can go on cleansing. . . . One of the intensest moments of my life was when I saw the force of that word '*cleanseth*'. The utterly unexpected and altogether unimagined sense of its fulfilment to me, on simply believing it in its fulness, was just indescribable. I expected nothing like it short of heaven.[13]

Grierson asserts that this key event in Havergal's spiritual life should be identified as a mystical experience, similar to those of Teresa of Avila or John of the Cross.[14] Yet it was more characteristic of the 'holiness movement' which was sweeping across Britain in the 1870s, associated with William Pennefather's Mildmay Conferences in north London and the Keswick Convention in the Lake District. Havergal happily associated with this movement, though she distanced herself from some of its excesses, like its teaching on sinless perfection. She was at pains to make clear: 'As to "perfectionism" or "sinlessness", I have all along, and over and over again, said I never did, and do not, hold either. "Sinlessness" belongs *only* to Christ now, and to our glorified state in heaven.'[15]

Five and a half years later, in May 1879, Havergal reiterated her dependence upon the precious blood of Jesus, as death drew near. From her bed, struck down by the agonies of peritonitis, she spoke on justification by faith: 'Not for our own works or deservings; oh, what vanity it seems now to rest on our own obedience for salvation, any merit of our own takes away the glory of the atoning blood. "Unto Him that loved us, and washed us from our sins in His own blood", *that's it.*' Her sister Maria asked, 'Have you any fear?', to which Frances replied, 'Why should I? Jesus said "It is finished", and what was His precious blood shed for? *I trust that.*' Later she added: 'I am sure "I am not worthy to be called His son", or His servant, but Jesus covers all; I am unworthy, but in Him complete.'[16]

Responding in Surrender and Service: 'All for Jesus'

Just a few weeks after the spiritual refreshing of December 1873, Havergal wrote a new hymn, 'From Glory unto Glory', about the blessings received through Christ and the complete surrender demanded by him. She declared that she could not have written these sorts of verses before:[17]

The fulness of His blessing encompasseth our way;
The fulness of His promises crowns every brightening day;
The fulness of His glory is beaming from above,
While more and more we realize the fulness of His love.

In full and glad surrender we give ourselves to Thee,
Thine utterly, and only, and evermore to be!
O Son of God, who lovest us, we will be Thine alone,
And all we are, and all we have, shall henceforth be Thine own.

Overwhelmed by the redeeming love of Christ, the theme of total
surrender came to dominate Havergal's later writings. She had long
emphasised the need for heartfelt response, as in one of her earliest
published poems, 'I Did This For Thee!' (1858), in which Christ asks the
reader, 'I gave My life for thee; What hast thou given Me?' Yet now 'All
for Jesus' and 'Only for Jesus' became constant refrains, or as she put it,
'not merely totality of surrender by exclusiveness of allegiance'.[18]

This theme is explored in her much loved 'Consecration Hymn',
written in February 1874 and based upon the post-communion prayer in
the *Book of Common Prayer*:

Take my life, and let it be
Consecrated, Lord, to Thee.

The hymn offers every part of life to God – time, hands, feet, voice, lips,
finance, intellect, will, heart and love – before ending with the couplet:

Take myself, and I will be
Ever, *only*, *all* for Thee.

It has even been suggested that Havergal's refusal of several suitors and
offers of marriage was a natural outworking of this total commitment to
God alone.[19] She wrote to a young friend:

Now I want you to be '*all* for Jesus'. I can't describe the happiness
He puts into any heart that will only give itself up altogether to
Him, not wishing to keep one single bit back. And I want you
to have this, and to have it *now*; not to wait till illness or great
trouble come, and you feel driven at last to Him. . . . Jesus says,
'Come *now!*' not, 'come when everything else has turned bitter'.
And if you come now, and surrender to Him now, you will have
the peace now and the gladness now; and I can tell you it is worth
having, because I *have* it, and so I *know* it is. It is a grand thing to
start out early, and be on the Lord's side all along.[20]

Havergal urged this same correspondent not to bring to Jesus 'just the
chips and shavings, the odds and ends' of her time and talents: 'Throw
overboard for ever the divided allegiance, which is valueless. Be "*only*
for Jesus", and you will start out on a new life of blessedness, beyond
anything you can imagine'.[21] Likewise she instructed a young man on
the eve of his twenty-first birthday:

you cannot serve two, much less several, masters. For, if you are serving self, and pleasure, and the world, even a little, you are serving Christ's enemy, and not serving Him really at all, because He accepts no divided service. . . . Oh, don't be afraid of taking the plunge, give yourself over into His hands . . . what blessedness you are on the edge of, if you would only give yourself 'in *full* and glad surrender' to Jesus. . . .[22]

Several of Havergal's poems develop this idea, such as 'Who is on the Lord's Side?' (1877) or 'Valiant for Truth' (1872) which begins:

Unfurl the Christian Standard! Lift it manfully on high,
And rally where its shining folds wave out against the sky!
Away with weak half-heartedness, with faithlessness and fear!
Unfurl the Christian Standard, and follow with a cheer!

It is also the repeated refrain of 'True-hearted, Whole-hearted' (1874):

True-hearted, whole-hearted, faithful and loyal,
King of our lives by Thy grace we will be
Under Thy standard, exalted and royal,
Strong in Thy strength, we will battle for Thee!

The poet commented:

One meets so many who only go such a little way; I mean really Christians, yet taking such faint interest in Christ's cause and kingdom, all alive as to art, or music, or general on-goings, yet not seeming to feel the music of His name. One does so long for all who are looking to Him for salvation to be 'true-hearted, whole-hearted'.[23]

Yet this loyalty to Jesus Christ was motivated by adoration as much as obligation. The themes of love and submission are frequently interwoven, as expressed in verses like 'O Saviour, precious Saviour, My heart is at Thy feet' and 'I love, I love my Master, I will not go out free!'[24]

One of the particular ways by which the Christian's whole-hearted devotion to Jesus should be evident, Havergal taught, was in evangelistic endeavour. Those following the Saviour should have an instinctive desire to tell others about him, as reiterated in her popular missionary hymns, 'Have You Not a Word for Jesus?' (1871) and 'Tell it Out' (1872). Havergal modelled this in her own life, through her regular cottage visiting, Sunday School teaching and personal counsel. For example, she pleaded with a friend: 'I want you for Jesus! . . . I do so long for you to give Him your heart and life now, so that you might never have the terrible sorrow of having only a death-bed to give Him! . . . There are so few comparatively that are on His side: won't you be one?'[25] She longed to be able to say, 'Another called, another brought, dear Master, to Thy feet!' and hoped that each new convert would in turn become an evangelist:

> Another voice to 'tell it out' what great things Thou hast done,
> Another life to live for Thee, another witness won.[26]

She was driven forward partly by her understanding that the most glorious rewards in heaven were reserved for those who 'Nearest to their Master trod, Winning wandering souls to God.'[27] Even in her final months, struggling with illness, Havergal started a Bible class amongst the labourers of Swansea, observing: 'I don't know who will come, few or many; but I want God's real converting grace poured out, and I want to be enabled so to speak of Jesus that souls may be won to Him.'[28]

Looking Forward in Hope: 'Near the Gates of Heaven'

Havergal suffered from persistent and debilitating illness throughout her adult life. Often she endured severe pain or enforced convalescence; sometimes she was brought to the verge of the grave before recovery. Her poetry at these periods is dominated by themes of trust in God's loving wisdom, submission to his good will, and a longing for the glories of heaven when all pain and suffering will cease. She tried to discern the lessons that God was teaching her through these trials (both spiritual and physical), as she wrote in her private journal:

> Oh that He may make me indeed a vessel 'sanctified & meet for the Master's use'. I look at trial & training of every kind very much in this light, not its effect upon oneself *for* oneself, but in its gradual *fitting* of me to do the Master's work. . . . Even in very painful spiritual darkness or conflict it has already sometimes comforted me to think that God might be leading me through strange dark ways so that I might sometime be His messenger to some of His children in similar distress.[29]

At a similar moment of difficulty, she observed: 'I have learned a real sympathy with others walking in darkness, and sometimes it has seemed to help me to help them.'[30] On occasion the agony was unbearable. One illness in the Swiss Alps in October 1876 brought forth 'A Song in the Night', with its startling affirmation, 'I take this pain, Lord Jesus, as Thine own gift'. She wrote to a friend: 'Pain, as to God's own children, is, truly and really, only blessing in disguise. It is but His chiselling, one of His graving tools, producing the likeness to Jesus for which we long.'[31] Elsewhere she affirmed, in one of her last poems before her death:

> Do what Thou wilt! Yes, only do
> What seemeth good to Thee:
> Thou art so loving, wise, and true,
> It must be best for me.[32]

Havergal was determined to 'Trust and obey!', confident that 'Though God's cloud-mystery enfold thee here, In after life and light *all* shall be plain and clear.'[33]

It was particularly the hope of heaven which helped the poet to persevere. As a girl, back in 1848, she had been comforted by her dying mother with the words: 'How glorious to know I shall soon see my Saviour face to face!'[34] Many years later, when it was her turn to comfort a bereaved child, Havergal similarly held out this vision of heaven:

> Jesus knows: knows exactly all you feel, has watched every tear, and listened, oh so lovingly, to every little cry. I think you must be in His very special care now, and He will give you, and *is* giving you, even *more* than all the care and love that your dear papa could give you. ... He is in Christ's safe keeping, and only think that, this very minute, he is seeing the King in His beauty, really seeing Jesus! Can you not be almost glad that he is seeing Him now? And he has really heard Jesus say to him, 'Well done, good and faithful servant; thou hast been faithful over a few things, I will make thee ruler over many things; enter thou into the joy of thy Lord.' Think how wonderfully happy it must have made him to hear his own dear Master's voice saying that to him![35]

Havergal herself longed for heaven. When she believed, incorrectly, that she had caught tuberculosis, her immediate reaction was one of joy: 'Oh the extraordinary thrill of delight the idea brought, that possibly I might be nearer heaven than I thought! It was almost ecstatic gladness; and then a chill of disappointment came when my common sense told me it could not be so!'[36] On another occasion, towards the end of 1874, she was genuinely struck down by typhoid fever, which almost proved fatal. Yet she professed herself unafraid to die and on the first day of her illness dictated to her niece a new poem beginning:

> Just when Thou wilt, O Master, call!
> Or at the noon, or evening fall,
> Or in the dark, or in the light,
> Just when Thou wilt, it must be right.

After recovering, she reflected:

> I never thought of death as going through the dark valley or down to
> the river; it often seemed to me a going up to the golden gates and
> lying there in the brightness, just waiting for the gate to open for
> me. . . . I never before was, so to speak, face to face with death. It
> was like a look into heaven; and yet, when my Father sent me back
> again, I felt it was His will, and so I could not be disappointed.[37]

Despite the lengthy illness, she was able to proclaim, 'it has been the
most precious year of my life to me', because of abundant proof of God's
presence and faithfulness.[38] She affirmed: 'I have not a fear or a flutter,
not a care or anxiety, for time or eternity'.[39] As a singer and songwriter,
Havergal eagerly anticipated joining with the heavenly music of the
angels in eternal adoration of the Saviour: 'The perfect harmony, the
perfect praise, no jarring tunes.'[40]

The end finally came in June 1879, when Havergal was just 42 years
old.[41] When the doctors informed her of the seriousness of this last illness,
she replied: 'I thought so, but if I am going it is too good to be true!' Again
and again in her final hours she called out, 'Splendid to be so near the gates
of heaven!' and 'So beautiful to go!' She asked for John Newton's hymn,
How Sweet the Name of Jesus Sounds, to be sung to her and declared: 'Oh,
it is the Lord Jesus that is so dear to me, I can't tell how precious! how
much He has been to me!' When the vicar of Swansea visited, to offer
words of comfort and counsel, he asked the dying Christian: 'You have
talked and written a great deal about the King; and you will soon see Him
in His beauty. Is Jesus with you now?' She replied:

> *Of course!* It's splendid! I thought He would have left me here a
> long while; but He is *so* good to take me now. . . . God's promises
> are all true, and the Lord Jesus is a good big foundation to rest
> upon. . . . Oh, I want all of you to speak *bright*, BRIGHT, words
> about Jesus, oh, do, *do!* It is all perfect peace, I am only waiting
> for Jesus to take me in.

Soon afterwards Havergal said: 'There is no bottom to God's mercy and
love; all His promises are true, not one thing hath failed.' As she took
her final breaths, many times she whispered, 'Come, Lord Jesus, come
and fetch me; oh, run, run.'

C.S. Lewis (1898-1963)

Michael Ward

When Lewis's autobiography *Surprised by Joy* appeared in 1955, many people turned eagerly to the account of his own conversion, hoping at last to have a glimpse of the personal reasons behind it, the reasons that counted for something in the silence of his own heart. The result was disappointment. The account is as lame and unconvincing as it could possibly be. All one brings away from it is the fact that it occurred at Whipsnade.[1]

So wrote the late John Wain, who was a junior member of Lewis's circle of friends, the Inklings, and later Professor of Poetry at the University of Oxford. His remarks are well worth considering because conversion narratives, especially adult conversion narratives which are climactic and dateable, like Lewis's, are often a good place to start an enquiry into the heart of a person's faith. The causes of the spiritual crisis, the circumstances surrounding it, and the immediate impact (theologically, socially, emotionally) upon the person concerned, often define for them their understanding of what it means to be a Christian. They start as they mean to go on. According to Wain, Lewis gave an unilluminating account of what stirred 'in the silence of his own heart' on that life-changing trip to Whipsnade Zoo. But is Wain right?

Surprised by Joy ends with a chapter entitled 'Beginning' in which Lewis records his transition from theism to Christianity in 1931. He writes:

I know very well when, but hardly how, the final step was taken. I was driven to Whipsnade one sunny morning. When we set out I did not believe that Jesus Christ is the Son of God, and when we reached the zoo I did. Yet I had not exactly spent the journey in thought. Nor in great emotion. 'Emotional' is perhaps the last word we can apply to some of the most important events. It was more like when a man, after long sleep, still lying motionless in bed, becomes aware that he is now awake. And it was, like that moment on top of the bus [when Lewis became aware that he was holding something spiritual at bay], ambiguous. Freedom, or necessity? Or do they differ at their maximum? At that maximum a man is what he does; there is nothing of him left over or outside the act. As for what we commonly call Will, and what we commonly call Emotion, I fancy these usually talk too loud, protest too much, to be quite believed, and we have a secret suspicion that the great passion or the iron resolution is partly a put-up job.

They have spoiled Whipsnade since then. Wallaby Wood, with the birds singing overhead and the bluebells underfoot and the Wallabies hopping all round one, was almost Eden come again.[2]

It is this passage which John Wain calls a 'disappointment . . . as lame and unconvincing as it could possibly be'. The reasons he gives for Lewis's 'inability to share his inner life', both in *Surprised by Joy* and throughout his writings, include Lewis's allegiances to the formality of the Edwardian age in which he grew up, his status as an Oxbridge don (for 'every don is equipped with a persona' behind which to hide) and his tendency, inherited from his lawyer father, always to be arguing a forensic case, using impersonal data and logic rather than revealingly personal, experiential evidence. Inhibited in all these ways, Lewis was unable to communicate the vital essence of his faith. His spiritual self-portrait is that of 'a wooden dummy', 'it bears the individual features of no living man'.

There is something in what Wain says. Lewis did tend deliberately towards a kind of impersonality in much of his work and it is helpful to bear this in mind when attempting to delineate the heart of his faith. What he chose to write about was not always necessarily what most resonated with him as an individual. For instance, in *Mere Christianity* his aim was to describe the broad central mainstream of the faith, rather than 'anything that was peculiar to the Church of England or (worse still) to myself'.[3] He took the same aim in *The Problem of Pain* where he attempts to assume 'nothing that is not professed by all baptized and communicating Christians'.[4] So anxious was he to distance his own personality from the arguments mounted in *The Problem of Pain* that, initially, he sought to publish the book anonymously, as indeed he had done with his first two volumes of poetry and as he would do with *A Grief Observed*, the journal-like description of his feelings of bereavement following the death of his wife. This self-effacement is to be found all over his work. In the allegorical account of his journey to faith, *The Pilgrim's Regress*, he tells the reader, 'you must not assume that everything in the book is autobiographical. I was attempting to generalize, not to tell people about my own life.'[5] In his *magnum opus* on the literature of the sixteenth century he assiduously avoids passing a theological verdict on the development of Protestantism ('it is not for the literary historian to say'[6]). And if he was determined to keep his own life and opinions off-stage in much of his work, he was equally determined as a critic not to treat poems, plays and novels as keys to their authors' personalities. In *The Personal Heresy* he argues that autobiographical details are irrelevant to a proper understanding of poetry: 'The poet is not a man who asks me to look at *him*; he is a man who says "look at that" and points; the more I follow the pointing of his finger the less I can possibly see of *him*.'[7]

Before we turn our attention back to that work in which one would have thought self-disclosure unavoidable, his conversion narrative, *Surprised by Joy*, it will be well to pause and reflect upon the situation we have just described. Lewis's avowed *im*personality should not be seen as an obstacle to our understanding of the heart of his faith: it is, in fact, part of that heart. There are two reasons for his studied determination not to wear his heart on his sleeve. The first has to do with his understanding of sin; the second has to do with his understanding of human consciousness.

First, sin. In *Surprised by Joy*, Lewis makes it clear that he was aware of his own identity as a sinner and gives numerous examples of how he succumbed to the temptations of 'the world, the flesh, and the devil'. As a schoolboy, he says, he laboured hard to make himself into 'a fop, a cad, and a snob'.[8] As a teenage student, he describes 'my deep-seated hatred of authority, my monstrous individualism, my lawlessness'.[9] And as a serviceman, he was bemused that some of his fellow officers should have been attempting 'strict veracity, chastity, or devotion to duty. I had taken it that they were not our subjects'.[10] At Oxford, when he examined himself seriously, he was appalled by what he found: 'a zoo of lusts, a bedlam of ambitions, a nursery of fears, a harem of fondled hatreds. My name was legion'.[11] It is always possible, of course, for public confessions to be a form of pride: they show how much a man thinks he can live without. However, one cannot help but sense that there is deep regret in the way Lewis recounts his mistreatment of his father, for example;[12] there is honest shame when he recalls how he received his first communion 'in total disbelief' – 'one of the worst acts of my life'.[13] Since he knew that his heart was, in the words of the prophet Jeremiah, 'deceitful above all things and desperately wicked', why would Lewis want to pay it much attention? He was impatient with fellow writers who could not get beyond 'the pageant of their own bleeding heart'.[14]

He thought them naïve and narcissistic. In Lewis's view, 'The real test of being in the presence of God is, that you either forget about yourself altogether or see yourself as a small, dirty object. It is better to forget about yourself altogether.'[15]

Lewis's close friend, Owen Barfield, homed in on this willed abdication of self-regard:

> At a certain stage of his life he deliberately ceased to take any interest in himself except as a kind of spiritual alumnus taking his moral finals . . . and I suggest that what began as deliberate choice became at length (as he had no doubt always intended it should) an ingrained and effortless habit of soul. Self-knowledge, for him, had come to mean recognition of his own weaknesses and shortcomings and nothing more. Anything beyond that he sharply suspected, both in himself and in others, as a symptom of spiritual megalomania.[16]

Barfield is close to the target here, but not exactly on the bull's-eye. It was not quite the case that Lewis considered self-knowledge to involve recognition of one's own weaknesses 'and nothing more'. No: there was a whole lot more, and it is important to emphasize that Lewis's low opinion of himself was different from a psychologically unhealthy self-loathing. For Lewis, self-knowledge involved such a deep recognition of one's weaknesses that it led to self-despair and a consequent unashamed dependency upon Christ. The grim initial diagnosis is made not out of perverse pleasure in cataloguing his faults and frailties; it is made with a view to attaining health, a new kind of health. It was essential to discover one's own moral 'bankruptcy',[17] and this could come about in no other way than by trying to keep God's law and failing. Only after a person attempts obedience and fails in the attempt does spiritual realism take root; only then (as he writes in *Mere Christianity*) do we 'change from being confident about our own efforts to the state in which we despair of doing anything for ourselves'.[18] 'Despair' is the key word here, as it is throughout Lewis's descriptions and depictions of conversion. In *The Voyage of the 'Dawn Treader'*, the obnoxious Eustace, having become a dragon and having found it impossible to shed his dragon skin himself, consents to be 'undragoned' by the Christ-like lion, Aslan, but only because 'I was pretty nearly desperate now.'[19] In *The Pilgrim's Regress*, the protagonist John 'shut his eyes, despaired, and let himself go',[20] as he dived head-first into the baptismal pool. Lewis's stance here is the same as that of St Paul in the Letter to the Romans who despairs at his inability to do the good he would and avoid the evil he would not: 'Wretched man that I am! Who will rescue me from this body of death?' Paul cries (Romans 7:24). One must be reduced to begging for help before one can become able to receive help. And because the help does indeed then arrive, the begging is retroactively transformed. The humiliation of having come to the end of one's own resources becomes, in hindsight, a *sweet* humiliation. It was not what one wanted, but it turns out to have been what one needed. And that is why Lewis can describe Christians in *The Four Loves* as 'jolly beggars';[21] or, as he puts it in *The Voyage of the 'Dawn Treader'*: 'It is better to be a beggar than a slave.'[22] Lewis's response to the discovery of his own helplessness is the same as that of Paul: 'Thanks be to God, through Jesus Christ our Lord' (Romans 7:25).

But if there is this retroactive transformation, why did Lewis remain so reluctant to pay attention to his own transformed life? Admittedly, there might be good reasons for not focusing upon the personality of an unredeemed sinner, but what about a personality recreated in Christ? We will find an answer if we look at Lewis's beliefs about human consciousness. This might seem a strange subject to consider when examining the heart of someone's faith. Should we not rather be thinking about something more obviously theological, such as his understanding of the cross of Christ or Scripture or the sacraments? For Lewis, this would be to put the cart before the horse. The person who has thoughts about the atoning sacrifice of Christ or about the Bible or about Holy Communion is a person thinking and knowing in one of two ways. And it is of fundamental importance that it should be principally one way rather than the other. Is it the way of Enjoyment or the way of Contemplation?

Lewis first encountered this distinction between Enjoyment and Contemplation in his mid-twenties in a book called *Space, Time and Deity* by the philosopher, Samuel Alexander. He was later to describe this antithesis as 'an indispensable tool of thought'[23] and he regarded it as so useful that he eventually wrote his own essay on the subject, 'Meditation in a Toolshed', in which he recast 'Contemplation' and 'Enjoyment' as follows:

> I was standing today in the dark toolshed. The sun was shining outside and through the crack at the top of the door there came a sunbeam. From where I stood that beam of light, with the specks of dust floating in it, was the most striking thing in the place. Everything else was almost pitch-black. I was seeing the beam, not seeing things by it.
>
> Then I moved, so that the beam fell on my eyes. Instantly the whole previous picture vanished. I saw no toolshed, and (above all) no beam. Instead I saw, framed in the irregular cranny at

the top of the door, green leaves moving on the branches of a tree outside and beyond that, ninety-odd million miles away, the sun. Looking along the beam, and looking at the beam are very different experiences.[24]

'Looking along the beam' is what Alexander had called 'Enjoyment' and 'looking at the beam' is what he had called 'Contemplation'. For Lewis, this distinction was so fundamental that he was prepared to divide conscious knowledge accordingly: 'Instead of the twofold division into Conscious and Unconscious, we need a three-fold division: the Unconscious, the Enjoyed, and the Contemplated.'[25] Like the ancient Persians who debated everything twice – once when they were sober and once when they were drunk – we should try out every experience in both lights, the light of Enjoyment (similar to the French *connaître*) and the light of Contemplation (similar to the French *savoir*).

And there is one experience which turns out to be much less Contemplatable than Enjoyable, namely the spiritual life of the Christian. The new identity or *novitas* which comes to the person baptised and reborn in the Holy Spirit is itself like a beam of light: 'In the Christian life you are not usually looking *at* Him [the Holy Spirit] . . . you have to think of the third Person as something inside you, or behind you.'[26] One cannot step outside one's new personality in Christ's Spirit because 'He is above me and within me and below me and all about me';[27] 'He is inside you as well as outside';[28] 'He is always both within us and over against us';[29] 'We may ignore, but can nowhere evade, the presence of God. . . . He walks everywhere *incognito*.'[30]

The Christian's relationship with God is inescapably participatory and 'looking along the beam' of that participation means inevitably that the beam is usually invisible. It is 'the actual presence, not the *sensation* of the presence, of the Holy Ghost which begets Christ in us. The *sense* of the presence is a super-added gift for which we give thanks when it comes, and that's all about it.'[31] Lewis quotes George MacDonald approvingly: 'The fool rejoices in his consciousness, instead of the life of that consciousness.'[32] Christ is the life of the Christian's consciousness: knowing him is incomparably more important than either knowing about him or knowing about the knower who knows him. As Lewis puts it in *Reflections on the Psalms*: 'There is no question of learning a subject but of steeping ourselves in a Personality, acquiring a new outlook and temper, breathing a new atmosphere.'[33]

Lewis's emphasis on the Enjoyability of Christ's Spirit helps explain why he so rarely got involved in debates between different Christian traditions. He seems to have thought that these differences arose from

Contemplating, rather than Enjoying. For instance, when it came to theories of the atonement (such as Ransom, Championship over Death, Substitution), he thought that to fix on any one of them as if it contained and limited the truth like a scientific definition, would be a mistake: the important thing was to be saved, not to have certain ideas about how salvation worked.[34] Likewise, with Scripture: one should not treat the Bible as a set of encyclopedic or encyclical proof-texts that could be applied to situations like patent remedies; rather, reading the Bible should be a process of 'steeping ourselves in its tone or temper'.[35] The same principle is to be found at work in his approach to Holy Communion. Lewis was not particularly interested in explanations about how the bread and the wine were the body and blood of Christ; he was interested that they were: 'The command, after all, was Take, eat: not Take, understand.'[36]

Of course, Lewis thought that there was a place for Contemplation (abstract, external, theoretical, uninvolved, observational, 'scientific' knowledge), but he regarded it as a subset of Enjoyment. The larger reality is the actual tasting of Christ's life, inhabiting it, allowing it to grasp and embrace one's whole being, including one's Contemplative intellect.

And it is of crucial importance to bear Enjoyment in mind when trying to understand the way Lewis describes his conversion in *Surprised by Joy*, for the sinful personality which there undergoes redemption is undergoing a redemption which is principally Enjoyed, not Contemplated. Lewis remarks that when he finally came to a belief that Jesus Christ is the Son of God there was 'nothing of him left over or outside the act'.[37] The whole man had moved. He had, as it were, stepped inside the 'beam' of Christian knowledge. He did not retain an 'angle' on God, a neutral perspective from which to survey his new faith. His new faith comprised his whole vision. As he put it in an interview with the Billy Graham Evangelistic Association: 'No part of you is outside the action.'[38] Likewise, his readers (if they are properly to understand the heart of his faith) should read his account of it in a manner which immerses their whole attention and sympathy and imagination.

At this point we would do well to remember how *Surprised by Joy* begins. It begins with Lewis explaining that, 'in a sense the central story of my life is about nothing else' than joy.[39] By 'joy' Lewis means eternal longing, *sehnsucht*, an inconsolable pang of yearning, a stab of awareness that one is not (yet) united to the divine heart of beauty, goodness and truth. Joy is, in this life, 'an unsatisfied desire which is itself more desirable than any other satisfaction.'[40] Joy, more than anything else, is what resonated deeply with Lewis at the centre of his own being, and the first chapter of his autobiography is carefully constructed so as to introduce it as the major theme.

He recounts how his earliest aesthetic experiences were incurably romantic and how once, in those early days, his brother had brought into the nursery the lid of a biscuit tin which he had covered with moss and garnished with twigs and flowers so as to make a toy garden or a toy forest. That was the first beauty Lewis says he ever knew: 'I do not think the impression was very important at the moment, but it soon became important in memory. As long as I live my imagination of Paradise will retain something of my brother's toy garden.'[41] Eight pages on and Lewis returns to this toy garden when describing his first real experience of joy:

> As I stood beside a flowering currant bush on a summer day there suddenly arose in me without warning, and as if from a depth not of years but of centuries, the memory of that earlier morning at the Old House when my brother had brought his toy garden into the nursery. It is difficult to find words strong enough for the sensation which came over me; Milton's 'enormous bliss' of Eden (giving the full, ancient meaning to 'enormous') comes somewhere near it. It was a sensation, of course, of desire; but desire for what? Not, certainly, for a biscuit-tin filled with moss, nor even (though that came into it) for my own past. . . . [B]efore I knew what I desired, the desire itself was gone, the whole glimpse withdrawn, the world turned commonplace again, or only stirred by a longing for the longing that had just ceased. It had taken only a moment of time; and in a certain sense everything else that had ever happened to me was insignificant in comparison.[42]

This is the origin of Lewis's pilgrimage, his quest for joy (or rather, as it turns out, Joy's quest for him) and we should keep it firmly in mind when we reach the end of the account and hear him describe what he felt when he arrived at Whipsnade, at last believing that Jesus Christ is the Son of God: 'Wallaby Wood with the birds singing overhead and the bluebells underfoot and the wallabies hopping all around one, was almost Eden come again.' There are birds overhead, there are flowers underfoot, there is abundant creativity in evidence on every side; above, below and around him he finds beauty, colour, and life. ('He is above me and within me and below me and all about me.') The 'enormous bliss' of Eden which accompanied Lewis's first taste of joy is now re-encountered, but this time with a difference. Eden is no longer a toy garden on a biscuit-tin lid that he could hold and look at from the outside: Eden is now a garden that holds him. Paradise has been regained, innocence recovered – or, at any rate, 'almost', for the consummation in heaven has yet to be attained. Nevertheless, the whole man had moved under or into the divine light: there was no residual spectator separate from the experience, outside the *novitas* beam.

Read like this, in the way it was intended to be read, so I believe, the account of what Lewis underwent at Whipsnade reveals itself as a profound and moving passage, and it admits us to the core of his faith: his sinful personality, his whole world, and his outlook upon it, have begun to be recreated in Christ, the second Adam, the true possessor of Eden. But it is easy to overlook the significance of the moment, not least because it is introduced with a distinctly downbeat sentence: 'They have spoiled Whipsnade since then.' This downplaying is part and parcel of Lewis's characteristic reticence explicitly to foreground himself. He was reticent for two reasons. First, because he wanted his readers to follow the pointing of his finger: the more they looked at the pointer, the less they would see where he pointed. And second, in attempting to describe his conversion, he was touching upon the most important encounter of his life, the tenderest and richest and most beautiful thing he ever experienced; it was not something that he was going to herald with drums and whistles. He expands on the causes of this hesitancy in his sermon, 'The Weight of Glory':

> In speaking of this desire for our own far-off country, which we find in ourselves even now, I feel a certain shyness. I am almost committing an indecency. I am trying to rip open the inconsolable secret in each one of you – the secret which hurts so much that you take your revenge on it by calling it names like Nostalgia and Romanticism and Adolescence; the secret also which pierces with such sweetness that when, in very intimate conversation, the mention of it becomes imminent, we grow awkward and affect to laugh at ourselves; the secret we cannot hide and cannot tell, though we desire to do both.[43]

Lewis could not hide his encounter with Christ in *Surprised by Joy*: to record that encounter was, after all, the main reason for writing his spiritual autobiography. On the other hand, he could not 'tell' it, either; it was too intimate, too deep, too precious to make overt and simple and 'accessible'; he was not going to cast his pearls before swine. And so he constructed the account with imaginative skill, with theological intelligence, and indeed, with artistic licence, in order to communicate the nature of the experience from the inside.[44] He gives an Enjoyable account of what had happened to him. He shows us, subjectively, what he addressed objectively in his apologetics: the transplantation of his heart, the acquisition of a new identity by one who did not deserve it:

> Until you have given up your self to Him you will not have a real
> self. . . . You must throw it away 'blindly' to so speak. Christ will
> indeed give you a real personality: but you must not go to Him
> for the sake of that. As long as your own personality is what you
> are bothering about you are not going to Him at all. . . . Look for
> yourself, and you will find in the long run only hatred, loneliness,
> despair, rage, ruin, and decay. But look for Christ and you will
> find Him, and with Him everything else thrown in.[45]

John Stott (born 1921)

David Wells

For over fifty years, John Stott served the same church. He was appointed rector of All Souls, Langham Place in central London in 1950, when he was only twenty-nine, and later became its rector emeritus in 1975. Though anchored to this one place during more than five decades, his visibility nevertheless steadily grew. He became a recognized leader in the resurgence of classic evangelicalism in the Church of England following World War Two, a prolific author, a frequent traveler, and a renowned preacher. Indeed, it would be true to say that in the second half of the twentieth century, few names stand out more prominently in the English-speaking church world than that of John Stott.

What motivated his influential ministry? What was his central concern? The answer, quite simply, is that Stott's deeply-rooted principles are insistently and self-consciously biblical. They make up a core of theological belief that has defined both his outlook and practice, how he sees himself and how he sees the world. Stott's Christian faith is *doctrinally* shaped and this is the ground on which he has stood in the Church of England. Its formal, doctrinal commitments are precisely those which are central to his evangelicalism. That is why, for many years, he preached annually on the Thirty-Nine Articles while at All Souls.[1] By the 1970s, other evangelical Anglicans were moving away from this confessional territory, but Stott never has.[2]

Evangelicalism has been defined from many different angles: historically, sociologically, generationally, culturally and, of course, theologically. It is the last of these ways that Stott himself adopted and this best explains his own inner core. Evangelical faith, he believed, is defined by three foundational truths and results in three defining characteristics. The truths are 'the authority of God in and through Scripture, the majesty of Jesus Christ in and through the cross, and the lordship of the Holy Spirit in and through his manifold ministries'.[3] It is the Father who reveals, the Son who dies in substitutionary atonement, and the

Spirit who transforms sinners by applying what the Son has achieved to them. From this Trinitarian work flow the characteristics which mark evangelical piety and practice. They are conversion, evangelism, and fellowship, each of which is wrought and sustained by God himself.

This was the understanding of evangelicalism which Stott reaffirmed to the two thousand delegates who met in Nottingham, in April 1977, for the Second National Evangelical Anglican Congress. There had been much discussion prior to the congress as to whether the word *evangelical* was still viable or useful. At the end of the congress, Stott endorsed the term, not because it had been used historically, and not out of any party spirit, but because of its affirmation of theological principle. Evangelical Anglicans, he said, were 'Bible people' and 'Gospel people' and thereby he reaffirmed the formal and material principles of historic Protestantism as being central to what it means to be evangelical and to be Anglican.[4] Let us consider Stott's understanding of these two principles.

'Bible People'

Revelation
It is impossible to think biblically about Christianity – to be 'Bible people' – without thinking in supernatural terms. It is a supernatural religion and 'we would know nothing about God if he had not made himself known'.[5] On this point, Stott saw himself taking the same position which Jesus had done in facing the Sadducees.[6] They were the sceptics of their day but we have their counterparts today, those who have difficulty believing that God has acted supernaturally in history.[7]

These supernatural acts are, of course, of different kinds. Key among them, though, are the ways in which God used the human language of the Bible to disclose his character, will, and acts to us.[8] Inspiration, Stott believed, is 'the concurrent operation of the divine Spirit and the human authors' such that their word is his.[9] This was the position that had been articulated for an earlier generation by B.B. Warfield – what Scripture says, God says.[10] And this conviction was central to the theology of the English reformers.[11] This sums up Stott's position, too, but with the caveat that Scripture must, of course, be interpreted aright. That is, it must be read in its own cultural and historical context first. Within this context, its language had its own particular meaning, and it must be understood within the conventions with which that language functioned. But, beyond that, we also need to see that the parts of Scripture belong within a whole so the parts cannot be given a meaning apart from, and in opposition to, the rest of Scripture. This is so because God is the author of it all and he does not contradict himself.[12]

Stott was willing to affirm that because of its inspiration, Scripture is 'without error in all that it affirms, and the only infallible rule of faith and practice.'[13] Because of its supernatural origin, it is uniquely authoritative and in this he was simply reiterating the reformers' insistence on *sola scriptura*. In the words of Article 20 of the Thirty-Nine Articles, it is not lawful for the church 'to ordain anything that is contrary to God's word written' or to set one Scripture against another. Scripture is authoritative because it brings us God's self-disclosure and not simply human ideas. It is, as a result, completely sufficient for a life of godliness in this world. This attitude toward Scripture, Stott believed, was that of Jesus, so 'submission to Scripture', he told David L. Edwards, is 'a sign of our submission to Christ'.[14]

Preaching
Preachers today no longer stand in the pulpit – if they use a pulpit at all – with the authority that they once did. Their status has declined considerably from the days when Charles Spurgeon's sermons, for example, made the news, not only in London, but the next day in New York and in Australia. In Stott's heyday, though, the power of his well crafted sermons, and the authority with which he preached, nevertheless made for remarkable hearing. As a preacher, J.I. Packer has said, Stott was 'expository, didactic, faithful, clear, weighty, masterful, exemplary.'[15]

The foundations for preaching are first and foremost theological. Theology, he said, is more important than methodology when it comes to preaching. Technique only makes orators, but without deep convictions of a theological kind no one becomes an effective preacher. These are the convictions about the nature and work of God, Scripture, the church, and the pastorate.[16] God has acted to reveal himself and has secured that revelation in Scripture; that Scripture is the truth he has given to the church; the church is dependent upon this word for its instruction and nourishment; and so it is the pastor's task to feed God's people. It was these very convictions which had restored preaching to its place of centrality in the church at the time of the reformation.[17] In this matter, there was a straight line that ran from Cranmer and Latimer to Stott.

And yet, there are many churches which are Protestant in name which are no longer Protestant in seeing the importance and centrality of preaching. The consequences are very evident today. 'The low level of Christian living is due', Stott said, 'to the low level of Christian preaching . . . the pew is a reflection of the pulpit.'[18] Low level preaching is preaching which has not the intent, or effect, of relaying the truth of God to his people. Perhaps, then, the most telling biblical image for preachers is that of the first-century steward. The steward was in a position of considerable responsibility, answerable to his master, but in charge of the household's provisions: 'If the steward is not expected to feed the household out of his own pocket, nor is the preacher to provide his own message by his own ingenuity.'[19] God has made all of the provisions for the feeding of the church in his word and all that the preacher is called to do is to serve that food. This is, as Cranmer and Latimer both said, the 'ordinary' means which God uses to draw sinners to himself, declare the gospel, and build up Christian understanding.

It is on these convictions that Stott became an exemplar of expository preaching. That is the kind of preaching which deliberately sets about opening up the meaning of a biblical text or passage for the congregation. 'The expositor', Stott wrote, 'prises open what appears to be closed, makes plain what is obscure, unravels what is knotted and unfolds what is tightly packed.'[20] The sole intent of this exercise is to bring the congregation face to face with the truth God has given to the church. More than that, it is to bring them face to face with the God of truth. How contradictory it is, then, when preachers shirk their responsibilities by inadequate preparation on the meaning of the text, or offer sermons that are shallow and thoughtless and so dishonour the God in whose household they serve as stewards.

Double Listening

Preaching, however, is not simply about making plain the meaning of the biblical passage. The point is also to make connections between that truth and the lives of those listening to the exposition. Preaching, Stott said, 'is not exposition only but communication'.[21] Initially, he spoke of this process under the image of 'bridge building'. As the years passed, this loomed larger in his mind. He began to speak more insistently about 'double listening', listening to the text and the people, listening so that the truth of the text could make the most effective connections with the lives of the people.

Stott worked diligently on understanding the other end of the text's trajectory, which is our modern world. Not only did he work with others on the matter of culture[22] but he also tackled some of the most pressing and thorny issues of the day like nuclear arms, poverty, the environment and unemployment.[23] And yet his own conceptual tools did not always help him to understand the world inhabited by the majority of Westerners. This is the world of democratic capitalism, of societies culturally dominated by large cities, of technology, mass communication, instant information, of affluence, of heightened levels of competition and of anxiety. Globalization today means not only that products move across national boundaries simply and easily, but so, too, do immigrants, nannies, sex workers, jihadists, fashion, foods, and almost anything that anyone is doing, or wants to do, anywhere in the world. The result is an open bazaar for ideas, worldviews, religions, and lifestyles where anyone can shop and where, when these views mingle together side by side, they tend to knock off each other's corners. They become options, only options, and the possibility of any one religion being uniquely true seems less and less likely. This is the world so many of Stott's listeners were actually inhabiting and into which he wanted to build his 'bridges' of truth, but this is probably the sphere where he struggled most to make successful connections.

'Gospel People'

Christ's Work

If evangelical Anglicans are 'Bible people', Stott had said at Nottingham, they are also 'Gospel people'. The way in which the gospel is conceptualized in his thought is rather chastely biblical but it also reveals some typically Lutheran interests. Indeed, Martin Luther is quoted approvingly a number of times in his writings. There is in Stott's thinking a moderate insistence on opposing law and gospel as well as on uniting all biblical motifs into an all-embracing Christ-centredness.[24] In fact, in Stott, both these typically Lutheran interests came together with a gentle Reformed celebration of divine sovereignty. This is not so surprising when one remembers that all the Thirty-Nine Articles have clear parallels in continental confessions of the reformation period, both Reformed and Lutheran.

So, where do we begin in thinking about the biblical gospel? We begin with the stark alternatives. Salvation, or acceptance with God, is either self-originated or divinely given. Those who think it can be self-originated, that it can be had by 'works', must reckon with law. The law, which encompasses all of God's commandments, is an expression of his righteous character and it brings its 'curse' upon all attempts at self-salvation. It does so because the consequence of a pervasively sinful human nature is that all fail. The 'dreadful function of the law is to condemn, not justify'.[25] Its function is not to offer a way of salvation but, by revealing sin, 'to convince men of their need of it'.[26] It is to convince people, in the words of Archbishop William Temple, that they contribute nothing to their salvation except the sin from which they need to be redeemed. This knowledge enables us to see that law and grace are the two divergent alternatives and that salvation is, from first to last, a divine gift. Salvation, as the reformers had argued, is *sola gratia*.

Stott insisted that it is impossible to understand either Christ aright, or the Bible aright, unless we have understood the cross aright. The cross was at the very centre of his thought because it is at the very centre of God's dealings with humanity, of his revelation of himself in Christ, and of his conquest over evil. The cross is made necessary by the gravity of sin, on the one side, and the wrath of God against it, on the other. 'God's holiness exposes sin', Stott wrote, 'his wrath opposes it'.[27] And if salvation cannot be had in self-terms, then it must be wrought through satisfaction in God's 'inner being' such that his character is satisfied, wrath is turned away from those who deserve it, and sinners are given a righteousness not their own.[28] This was accomplished through Christ's substitution for and in place of sinners, the just for the unjust. Christ, he writes, 'took our curse, so that we might receive his blessing; he became sin with our sin, so that we might become righteous with his righteousness'.[29] There could be no atonement without substitution. And this substitution of Christ in our place had to be penal as he absorbed in himself the consequences of our lawbreaking.[30]

Gospel and Spirit

The work of Christ on the Cross was unique in its accomplishment, decisively finished in the past, and it is objective to us. The work of the Spirit is subjective, ongoing, and never completed in us until the day of our death. It is the Spirit's work to take what Christ has done and apply this to us.

This application begins in regeneration which 'is entirely a work of God', Stott explains, and it precedes conversion, 'the turning from sin and to God in Christ by faith'.[31] This new birth is necessary and without it there is no Christian faith in biblical terms. And regeneration is not synonymous with baptism. Regeneration is, though, the beginning of a life of holiness, which is impossible without the Holy Spirit. It is the Spirit who brings home the truth of God's word so that sinners respond to it 'in penitence, faith and obedience.'[32] And it is the Spirit who progressively transforms believers into Christ's image, empowering them to live like him in this world. Stott rejected the Pentecostal position, and that of the earlier Keswick movement, that the work of the Spirit comes in two discernable stages, first regeneration and then, in a second stage, a deeper and more thorough sanctifying or Spirit-filled moment. It is difficult 'to resist the conclusion', he said in reference to 1 Corinthians 12:13, 'that the baptism of the Spirit is not a second and subsequent experience enjoyed by some Christians, but the initial experience enjoyed by all.'[33]

Gospel and Sacraments
In his death, Christ made a full, complete and sufficient sacrifice for sin. It is the purpose of the Lord's Supper to set forth visually what Christ accomplished on the cross. It is an outward and visible sign of an inward and spiritual grace, as the old Anglican catechism defines it. That was Stott's view. There can be no legitimate references to a reenactment of this sacrifice. Nothing can duplicate what Christ has done, or repeat it, still less substitute for what he accomplished. And the same can be said of baptism, the only additional sacrament which Stott recognized. It is not itself regenerative, nor the means of regeneration, but simply the representation and symbol of regeneration as the child is welcomed into the local church.[34]

Gospel and World
As Stott's ministry grew internationally, initially as a missioner to universities in the British Commonwealth, especially in the 1960s and 1970s, and then later as teacher and preacher in churches, his own understanding of the world was also greatly expanded. In the Third World especially, he encountered a church whose pastors were sometimes untrained, who had no resources of study, and who ministered to many who were impoverished, the victims of corruption, of massive governmental failure sometimes, and of untreated diseases. How can one preach the gospel to those who are hungry, or are on the margins of society, without making their physical needs a part of one's Christian outreach?

In 1975, Stott published his *Christian Mission in the Modern World*, a simple book but also a pioneering accomplishment. He argued that evangelism and social responsibility belong together. Their relationship varies according to the circumstances. Sometimes social responsibility is a consequence of evangelism because it is the expression of new life in Christ. Sometimes it is a bridge for evangelism as it gains a hearing for the gospel. And sometimes it is a partner of evangelism as deeds of compassion confirm the words by which the gospel is made known. In no way is social responsibility itself the gospel; nor should the gospel stand alone where human need cries out for Christian compassion.

This formulation revealed disagreements on both sides of the ecumenical debate. To those in the World Council of Churches, Stott argued that the gospel of Christ's penal substitution cannot be subsumed under social responsibility nor is the gospel itself about political liberation.[35] To those on the evangelical side, Stott was at pains to say that what he proposed was not the old, liberal social gospel that some feared.[36] In the end, evangelicals who had been divided on this issue came together around the proposal Stott had first formulated in 1975.[37]

Conclusion

There can be no doubt that John Stott was given, at birth, an unusual set of abilities: a brilliant mind, calm disposition, natural leadership, and a warm, winsome personality. Yet these gifts might well have been put to work in ways other than those of Christian ministry. As it turned out, under the hand of God, these extraordinary gifts were harnessed by the truth of Scripture and put in service of the Christ who is at the heart of that revelation. Simple as this sounds, it is the explanation of John Stott's extraordinary ministry.

David Watson (1933-1984)

Graham Cray

David Watson was the most gifted and effective English evangelist of his generation. As an evangelist, teacher and author he reached large numbers of people across the English-speaking world and beyond. At the peak of his ministry (based at St Michael-le-Belfrey Church in the centre of York) he identified three priorities – evangelism, renewal and reconciliation. Each was close to his heart, but evangelism exercised a clear priority.[1] Renewal and reconciliation in the church were essential if the church was to preach the gospel effectively and without hypocrisy. Watson was well aware of the prevalence of a Jesus 'yes', church 'no' mentality.[2] But he knew that conversion was into the church, hence his commitment to renewal: 'At heart, I am profoundly concerned for the spiritual renewal of the church, which I see to be essential for effective mission in the restless and dangerous age in which we live.'[3] Equally the body of Christ 'torn from limb to limb' could not display Christ as it should – hence the necessity of reconciliation.[4]

Before identifying the theological convictions that sustained these core aspects of his vocation, we should note that it is fitting for this chapter to follow the one concerning John Stott. Watson was led to Christ as a Cambridge undergraduate in October 1954 by John Collins, at that time Stott's curate. He was nurtured in the faith by David Sheppard, later Bishop of Liverpool, and through them introduced to the public school camps at Iwerne Minster, led by the Revd Eric Nash ('Bash'), through whom Stott had also become a Christian. Stott invited Watson to serve his curacy at All Souls, Langham Place although it was Collins' invitation to St Mark's, Gillingham which he eventually accepted. Theologically, and in similarity of background, Watson was a Stott-shaped evangelical, holding the core convictions of 'Bible people' and 'Gospel people' as Stott articulated them. Although the two men differed over the charismatic movement, Watson never lost his great respect for Stott and always carefully read his books.

Watson stood within the Anglican evangelical mainstream, above all as a Scripture person, while consistently challenging (and in his own life trying to break free from) the constraints of its public school ethos and some of its theological blind spots. Watson's biographers, Saunders and Sansom, capture his methodology well: 'As always when he received fresh insights, he began to submit these to the scrutiny of Scripture and to try to express them in realistic and practical terms for the benefit of others.'[5]

The Holy Spirit

Scripture was always central to Watson's theology: 'Although God is by definition our final authority, the Bible is our final court of appeal for what God has said. Here is the God-given objective test for our belief and behaviour.'[6] But the Bible's teaching about the Holy Spirit included an experienced encounter. The personal hunger for God, which led to Watson's initial conscious experience of being filled with the Holy Spirit, was fostered through several months of study of the Beatitudes.[7] The activity of the Holy Spirit ('the key to everything in the New Testament Church')[8] as the transforming power of God was central to his ministry.

Although a leader in the charismatic movement, Watson never accepted a Pentecostal, two-stage theory of encounter with the Spirit. He was also uncomfortable with the way the term 'baptism in the Holy Spirit' was often used. To him this was obviously initiation language, and could not be disconnected from regeneration, yet it also implied an experienced reality. He took up a position midway between the writings of John Stott and Martyn Lloyd-Jones, typically attempting to identify some common ground. All Christians had received the Holy Spirit, but not all Christians were filled with the Holy Spirit. He was particularly challenged by some words of Lloyd-Jones: 'Got it all? Well, if you have "got it all" I simply ask, in the name of God, why are you as you are? If you have got it all, why are you so unlike the New Testament Christians?'[9] The most important issue was to understand the full scope of God's gift in Christ and to live in the full reality of it. The Holy Spirit was the key to both.

This was absolutely integral to Watson's work as an evangelist: 'It is useless to attempt to witness to Christ, in obedience to his command, without the power of his Spirit. . . . Anyone can preach words; some can preach convincing and persuasive words; but only God can change lives.'[10] In other words, to obey the scriptural command to witness, without a conscious dependence on the work of the Holy Spirit, is not to obey the Scriptures. Renewal and evangelism were inseparably linked:

> There is nothing so inspiring as seeing God at work. When men and women are won for Christ, when lives are changed (sometimes dramatically so), when Christians give generously and spontaneously to God's work, when some are healed of sickness and others delivered from demonic powers, when there is a glorious sense of God's presence in the praise of his people, when there is an almost tangible experience of the love of God within the body of Christ. . . . That is why spiritual renewal is so vital to evangelism.[11]

The dispute over the term 'baptism in the Holy Spirit' eventually led him to review his own framework for leading people to Christ. At his conversion Watson had used the prayer in John Stott's *Becoming a Christian* (1950), based on Revelation 3:20.[12] Like many others he invited the Lord and Saviour to 'come in' to his life, but this prayer made no mention of the Spirit. In contrast, during his own evangelistic ministry Watson called upon his hearers to Repent, Believe and Receive – repent of their sin, believe in (and surrender to) Christ, and receive the Holy Spirit.[13]

Emotion and 'emotionalism' were strongly discouraged in Iwerne-shaped Christianity. Bash did not permit 'emotional prayers'.[14] Watson never encouraged emotion for emotion's sake. He never treated emotion as a trustworthy evidence of the Holy Spirit, and encouraged those who prayed to be filled with the Spirit to trust God's written promise.[15] But the presence of the Spirit could not be restricted to a doctrinal conviction that he was present: 'For too long we have over-intellectualised the Christian faith, reducing much of it to the level of words and propositions.'[16] The Spirit was an experienced reality. This was a period, in the 1970s and early 1980s, when many people began to explore a more holistic understanding of human identity, an integration of body, mind and emotion. The Spirit of God engaged with the whole person.

Watson never allowed 'experience' to supplant the authority of Scripture, but he did believe that experience can help us to see Scripture differently, and open our eyes to truths in Scripture which we had not previously recognised. He had been taught as a young Christian that the New Testament charismatic gifts were restricted to the time of the apostles. But his encounter with those gifts made this an untenable position: 'The more I studied the New Testament the more I became convinced: the teaching that these gifts were only for the apostolic age was no more than a rationalisation of their absence for so long.'[17]

Rather the gifts were the way in which 'Jesus by his Spirit works through his body', 'not a static, permanent possession, but . . . given as an expression of God's present activity when the need arises.'[18] This rediscovery of the Spirit's gifts, and of the miraculous, was always kept in perspective with the greatest miracle – conversion was the supreme supernatural work of the Spirit: 'We must never devalue the miracle of the new birth.'[19]

Watson would have liked Gordon Fee's description of the Spirit as 'God's Empowering Presence'.[20] His understanding of the Spirit as the presence of God also profoundly shaped his understanding of worship, which he regarded as 'the primary task of the church'.[21] He insisted that 'true worship' must always be directed towards the living God, always edify the body of Christ, and that it 'always depends on the presence of the Holy Spirit'.[22] This powerfully influenced Watson's approach to public evangelism. In all his city wide missions (known as festivals) preaching took place in the context of worship, involving song, dance, drama and mime. The whole person was invited to engage with God: 'on many occasions I have seen the close link between the praise of God, when marked by the freshness and freedom of the Spirit's presence, and powerful evangelism.'[23] Watson understood from Scripture that the church always needed renewal, not just to turn from sin, or awake from sleep, or even to regain the full reality of New Testament Christianity, but also to keep in step with the Spirit. 'The Spirit of God . . . is the Spirit of movement', so the church had to be much more a movement than an institution.[24]

The Body of Christ

The pattern of faith to which Watson was introduced as a young convert tended to be individualistic. While emphasizing the importance of fellowship it did not much allow for the fundamentally relational nature of Christian discipleship. The church as the body of Christ, or the family of God, characterised by mutual committed relationships, became central to Watson's teaching and practice.[25] Many evangelists hold lightly to the church, concentrating on winning new people to faith. But Watson wrote a major book on the subject, *I Believe in the Church* (1978), at a time when few evangelical authors gave it any attention. Once again experience had helped throw new light on Scripture. *I Believe in the Church* is profoundly biblical, because it is full of insights learned by a pastor. He wrote what he had taught his congregation at St Michael-le-Belfrey to live.

Watson's personal hunger for God had led to his encounter with the

Spirit. That personal encounter quickly led to the discovery that the gifts of the Spirit were for today. This moved the spotlight from individual experience to mutual ministry. Each needed the ministry of the others. Gifts from God were to be received via fellow Christians. Only in this way could the church grow to maturity. Just as Watson's understanding of the work of the Spirit emphasized the need to grow into the reality of all that had been given in principle at conversion, so also in the life of the local church. Renewal was not just restoration from inadequate forms of church life, it was a lifelong growth into the fullness of Christ. This discovery of the renewing role of the Spirit gave rise to and then undergirded a well developed ecclesiology:

> Each individual *ekklesia* (local church, groups of churches or denomination) is not *the* church, but *fully represents it* ... the *whole* gospel, the *fullness* of God, the *finished* work of Christ together with the 'immeasurable greatness' of his resurrection power, the *complete* gift of the Holy Spirit together with the full range of his gifts and ministries, and the 'very great promises' of God offering *full* salvation – all these are available in every place, wherever the church, great or small, is to be found.[26]

The ministry of each member of the body was essential to the body. When visitors asked, 'Who is the minister of this church?', Watson suggested the reply, 'We all are.' This scriptural conviction led to the restructuring of the whole congregation at St Michael-le-Belfrey into small groups, where each could minister to the others. It also led to an understanding that leadership has to be shared. An 'eldership', or mixed team of lay and ordained, became an early norm.[27]

But if the reality of spiritual gifts led initially to the understanding of the church as the body of Christ, it was the central place given to mutual committed relationships which created the environment in which gifts could be received, encouraged and exercised. Christians belong to one another because they are 'in Christ'. Unity is a fruit of the cross: 'The true basis for all fellowship is when two or more persons kneel at the foot of the cross of Jesus Christ, trusting wholly in his mercy and love.'[28] Those who receive the love of God in Christ are to respond to that love, not only by loving God, but by loving one another: 'The Bible ... is insistent that our love for God, although intensely personal, is not to be private. It is to be seen in the love we show towards one another.'[29] This love is enabled and matured by the work of the cross and of the Spirit.

Scripture and the Holy Spirit were the key resources which shaped and reshaped St Michael-le-Belfrey. (A visiting analyst identified an unusually high degree of openness to change when he researched the congregation.) The DNA of the congregation was love: 'It is only God's love, given to us by his Spirit, that will ever make community possible.'[30] Foremost, this was love for Christ, of course, 'But if this love for Christ is to mean anything at all, it must spill over into love for other people, especially for our brethren in Christ.'[31] This quality of Spirit-empowered relationship became the seedbed of everything else. Within these relationships gifts were exercised for the first time: 'It is as we live together in love that the Spirit will give his gifts as an expression of his love within his body, the church.' Within these relationships believers found healing from the past and growth in holiness. Within these relationships artistic gifts emerged as songs, dances, dramas and banners were created. Through these relationships lives could be lived more simply, and resources released for the work of the kingdom and care of the poor.[32] The local church became a crucible for learning to love, an environment in which love developed and could be given away in evangelism and service. The church's relationships gave integrity to its public claims and external ministry.[33]

Watson travelled with a team so that he could demonstrate in his wider ministry the fruit and reality of what God was doing at home. In effect he took 'church' on the road: 'The reality of Christ can often be seen best in our corporate life. . . . Renewal affects the body of Christ, not just the individual. . . . Worship is our foremost priority, and I want to set evangelism firmly in the context of worship. In this way we may be better able to hear God's word.'[34] The last sentence is important. This was not a ministry which under emphasized the preaching of Scripture, but one which set that preaching in a context which Scripture itself described.

Given this corporate emphasis, it should not be surprising that to this public ministry of evangelism and renewal Watson added a third cord, that of reconciliation. Division within the body of Christ was a scandal and tragedy which impeded the work of the gospel. *One in the Spirit* (1973) was written to address division, not just to set out a personal stance. Neither racial division in South Africa nor Protestant / Roman Catholic division in Northern Ireland could be left unchallenged. At the National Evangelical Anglican Congress at Nottingham in April 1977, Watson went so far as to declare that the reformation was a tragedy (despite the biblical truths that it rediscovered) because 'from the Reformation onwards the Body of Christ in the world has been torn from limb to limb into hundreds of separate pieces.'[35] One vital dimension of scriptural truth had been regained at the price of another.

Vulnerability and Suffering

Watson's emphasis on relationships led him to value vulnerability in a way that was incomprehensible to some of his Iwerne mentors. To be vulnerable was not to be emotional or introspective, it was to open oneself to God's transforming grace through others:

> When I am willing to be open to you about my own personal needs, risking your shock or rejection, and when I am willing for you to be equally open with me, loving you and accepting you with unjudging friendship, we find ourselves both at the foot of the cross, where there is level ground, at the place of God's healing and grace.[36]

Watson modelled this by striking frankness about his asthma, his occasional depressions and the sometimes stormy nature of his marriage to Anne ('She's stubborn and I'm determined!'). This public honesty (like that of St Paul in 2 Corinthians 1:3-11, 12:1-10) opened people up to the word of God. The response of his audience was often, 'If God can help him, then perhaps God can help me.'

The new lessons learned in York involved a painful 'unlearning' of previous ways of thinking and behaving. Renewal cannot be cheap grace. Watson once said that the fellowship's history could be summed up as 'joy and pain are woven fine'.[37] In *Discipleship* (1981) he explained:

> We are called, as disciples of Christ to share our lives together, and, if need be, our possessions together. We are to open our hearts to one another, take off our masks, becoming real and honest. And when fellowships of Christians try seriously to do this in the power of the Holy Spirit, they will soon discover two things. First, they will discover deep and loving relationships as brothers and sisters in Christ. . . . But second, they will also find pain, since we are still angular and sinful persons who . . . hurt and jab one another.[38]

Once St Michael-le-Belfrey went through a painful split. There was and is a price to renewal by the word and Spirit.

It is not possible to write about Watson's central convictions without considering his attitude to impending death from cancer:

> The Kingdom has come now, since Christ has come to be our Saviour and King; but it will not yet be consummated until Christ comes again with power and glory. Even where healings are experienced widely not all sick people are healed. Christ taught us to pray 'Your Kingdom come', and we are still to wait with patience for what we see only in part at present.[39]

Fear No Evil (1984), published shortly after his death, is an extraordinary book which holds both the 'already' and the 'not yet' in a faith-filled tension. Like all of Watson's most creative work it brings together Scripture and experience. In the experience of terminal cancer, a man who believes in, and has seen, the healing power of Christ, engages the problem of suffering, refusing triumphalistic short cuts. The arguments do not cover every possible dimension of the problem, nor rebut every possible objection. The tensions are not all resolved (and will not be in this life), but shining through it all is the hope of heaven. The 'already', that is the reality of all that has been experienced of Christ by the Spirit, is a foretaste and promise of the 'not yet'. This is true in personal experience: 'When I die, it is my firm conviction that I shall be more alive than ever, experiencing the full reality of all that God has prepared for us in Christ. Sometimes I have foretastes of that reality, when the sense of God's presence is especially vivid.'[40] But it is also true corporately: 'To experience the godly love of God's family is one of the most treasured riches for those in Christ. If heaven is like this, only much more so, why are we so reluctant to go there?'[41] Christ's triumph has reduced the fear of death to the fear of dying: 'As a Christian I believe, not just in life *after* death, but in life *through* death.'[42] In his penultimate sermon, in January 1984, Watson proclaimed: 'Even death itself is not a threat.'[43] The dying Christian was still the living evangelist. *Fear No Evil* contains teaching on the reality of spiritual death, and the danger of eternal death, together with a concise statement of God's remedy in Christ. At the heart of biblical Christian faith is hope, rooted in the finished work of Christ. This is a theological hope, but it must also be a personal hope. It must be both taught and lived. David Watson embodied the two. In his final days he affirmed, 'The best is yet to be' and 'There is nothing that I want more than to go to heaven. I know how good it is.'[44]

A Forerunner

At the memorial service in York Minster, Archbishop Stuart Blanch described Watson as 'a burning and shining lamp', comparing him to John the Baptist.[45] Watson was indeed a forerunner. His commitment to Scripture and his openness to the Spirit, at a time of major cultural change, enabled him to pioneer a range of developments which are taken as normal today. He championed a more holistic view of Christian life and ministry, and of the human person. He reconnected evangelism and the church. He emphasized the essentially corporate nature of Christian discipleship. He re-engaged evangelicals with the arts and brought a charismatic dimension to the struggle for Christian unity. He engaged with the challenges of global poverty without abandoning his core calling as an evangelist. He embraced Christ's ministry of healing, while facing death from cancer with the hope of heaven. He was 'a burning and shining lamp' whose light prepared the way for future generations.

Epilogue:
The Apostolic Teaching and Anglicanism

Michael Nazir-Ali

It is not at all an exaggeration to say that my heart has been warmed as I have read about these great men and women, in the Anglican tradition, who have been witnesses to the faith of the apostles.

It is true, of course, that this tradition has arisen and has flourished in these islands in a particular way and something of the temper and the flavour of the culture, customs, habits and language of the peoples here has attached itself to the tradition. Anglicanism has also spread widely throughout the world, sometimes along with British imperial interests and at other times contrary to them. It has spread to countries like Korea where Britain has certainly *not* been the imperial power and to Japan which undoubtedly has harboured imperial ambitions. It is quickly becoming a significant reality in Francophone Africa and some of its fastest growing churches are in former Portuguese territories.

Whilst most Anglicans respect the Anglican Communion's English origins, these are not the main reason why they are Anglican. If asked why they are Anglican, they would say that it was because through this tradition they have been brought to a living faith in Jesus Christ, been empowered by the Holy Spirit and experienced something of the continuity of Apostolic Teaching down the ages and throughout the world. In other words, barring a relatively few Anglophiles, the reason they are Anglican has not so much to do with Anglicanism's origins as with its apostolicity. The church cannot be simply the expression of the religiosity of a people, whether they are from England or elsewhere. It must strive to be authentically apostolic and its relationship with culture must be determined by this commitment.

It is well-known that the Anglican reformers did not claim any peculiar doctrines as their own. They simply wanted their church to be fully and purely apostolic. They wanted it to be an example of the famous Vincentian Canon: *quod ubique, quod semper, quod ab omnibus creditum est* ('What has been believed everywhere, always and by all'). Such a commitment has meant taking seriously how the apostolic teaching has been given, received and passed on down the generations and across the globe. It is true, of course, that at different times and in different cultures elements of this teaching, for example about holiness or healing or the place of the poor or of women, have received particular attention in particular contexts. This is only to be expected and will continue as the gospel comes into contact with the aspirations, values and worldviews of various cultures. When, however, it is asked whether some development or other is authentically apostolic teaching the question has always been settled by an appeal to the Holy Scriptures. Authentic development of doctrine is not ruled out but it must be such as brings out the implications of the apostolic teaching for a particular situation, which makes the gospel clearer and shows the continuity of the church's teaching down the ages and across the world.

This is the reason why the Scriptures have been studied so reverently and assiduously by Anglicans. They have wanted to know how these precious documents came to be. What are the oral and written traditions behind them? What were the immediate circumstances and motivations of those who wrote or edited them? And all of this to discover how God speaks to us in and through the Bible. Anglican scholars have wanted to get 'behind the text' to better understand the background to a particular book or passage. They have given close attention to what is 'in the text', to the language; its grammar, etymology and history, as well as to its literary aspect. And then they have related all of this to what is 'in front of the text': the culture and the context to which the Bible is brought and where it is read and acted upon.

It is extremely important for God's word to be expressed and lived in a way which is intelligible and transparent in every culture. This is not just a matter of Bible translation (important as that is). It has to do with a people's response in terms of how they worship, how they celebrate their faith and how they communicate with those who are still outside the community of faith. Once again the foundation documents of Anglicanism, whether the *Book of Common Prayer* or the Articles of Religion, provide a basis for engaging with culture which takes seriously the 'tongue understood of the people' (Article 24) and also 'the diversities of countries, times and men's manners' (Article 34). In many places, such an engagement with culture in terms of the church's worship, structures and ministries (in accordance with the aspirations of the Chicago-Lambeth Quadrilateral) has hardly begun to take place. At the same time, it needs to be stressed that the gospel cannot simply be made 'captive' to a particular people and their way of life, nor can the church just 'capitulate' to what is contemporary with it.

One of the reasons for the present 'crisis' in the Anglican Communion is a failure to discern the difference between a proper inculturation of the good news, which is a necessity in the church's mission, and an improper capitulation, which makes it impossible for the church to be prophetic in the face of whatever is contrary to that fullness of life which is God's purpose for us. Nothing in the church's engagement with *any* cultural context can be allowed to compromise the very nature of the gospel: for example, the Bible's analysis of the human condition, God's purposes as shown in his dealings with his people, the person and work of Christ, and the Christian hope for the renewal of the whole of creation which is based on the resurrection of Jesus from the dead. In any such encounter, there will be both judgement and fulfilment. The proclamation of the good news will, of course, bring to light all that is wrong in people's lives but it will also fulfil their deepest aspirations such that Christ is shown to be the centre of all that is true, good and beautiful in their particular story. From an ecclesial point of view, nothing in the process of inculturation should destroy, or even damage, fellowship among Christians and churches of different cultures. Each must be able to recognise the gospel in the life and witness of the other. The good news then of God's saving purposes and work needs to be expressed in the language, idiom and thought-forms of every culture so that it can be understood, accepted and lived. It is certainly true that there will be trajectories in the Bible and, more generally, in the story of God's people which will resonate particularly with this or that group because of their background or context. The Exodus trajectory, for instance, has always appealed to enslaved, oppressed and marginalised groups. The events of Exile and Return speak especially to refugees and to those who, for one reason or another, have become alienated from their origins. At the same time, it is important to stress that the whole of the biblical witness should be available to people and brought to bear on their circumstances. We cannot simply pick'n'mix whatever it is that suits us and discard the rest.

The necessity of maintaining, enhancing and (sometimes) restoring fellowship among the churches raises the question of the relationship between unity and diversity. If culture is to be taken seriously, there will be many different expressions of Christian life, worship, church structures and forms of ministry. This is as it should be but then we have to ask what, if anything, holds Christians together, what are the limits of diversity and can we distinguish between legitimate and illegitimate claims? The nineteenth-century American Episcopalian theologian, William Reed Huntington, in his book *The Church Idea: An Essay Towards Unity* (1870) distinguished between what he called the Anglican system and the Anglican principle. The former has to do with the 'picturesque costume' which English church life has thrown around the latter, which should be the focus of our attention. Huntington believed that at the heart of the principle was the calling of the local church to be and to become the catholic church in its locality. Huntington was, however, too committed an ecumenist not to realise that this can happen only when a particular local church is in fellowship with all the other local churches. In this sense, he anticipated the teaching of the New Delhi Assembly of the World Council of Churches (1961): 'all in each place united with all in every place and age'. As a basis for such unity he proposed a Quadrilateral which was, subsequently, adopted by the House of Bishops of the American Church and, later, by the Lambeth Conference of 1888. The Quadrilateral sets out the Scriptures as the norm of Christian believing, the catholic creeds as a sufficient statement of the Christian faith, the dominical sacraments as means of grace and the historic ministry as the basis for promoting Christian unity. It would not be an exaggeration to say that the Quadrilateral has been hugely significant in the emergence and development of modern ecumenism. It was, of course, always at the centre of any church union schemes in which Anglicans were involved and it is impossible to imagine the sort of convergence on ministry that is shown, for example, in the Lima text *Baptism, Eucharist and Ministry* (1982) without thinking also of the Quadrilateral.

What is, perhaps, not always understood so clearly is that the Quadrilateral, apart from being a charter for greater Christian unity, is also a statement of Anglican identity and a summary of the basis for Anglican unity. It cannot, of course, be *all* that is required for maintaining and promoting unity in the church. For that, we also need anointed and authentic teachers of the word of God who will bring out its implications for Christian living today. The so called 'instruments of Communion' whether it is the Lambeth Conference of Bishops or the Primates of the Communion or any other instrument need to see themselves in this light. At the same time, we must remember that the gospel provides all that the church requires in order to flourish. Teaching, prophetic, pastoral and missionary offices should all spring from the gospel, which forms the church. They cannot simply be invented to meet this or that contingency. If Anglicanism is truly apostolic, we have to ask why these offices have not always functioned effectively. Has the Erastian inheritance of Anglicanism 'muffled' or 'hobbled' the full, apostolic expression of all the church should be?

The good news of Jesus is about the restoration and healing of human beings as individuals but it is also about the ordering of the community which comes into being as people are saved and incorporated into the Body of Christ, the church. The gifts of each have to be recognised and nurtured for the sake of the whole. Those with responsibility for speaking in the name of Christ, the head of the body (Article 26), must be able to exercise their God-given ministry freely and without hindrance. The church's unity, catholicity, apostolicity and holiness are, of course, maintained by regular and Spirit-filled worship, by the faithful teaching of God's word and by the due celebration of the sacraments but they are also maintained by the holiness of Christian living and, where necessary, by godly discipline which is merciful but firm. Because of the perceived burdensomeness of the minutiae of medieval discipline, there was an extensive debate at the time of the reformation about the place of discipline in the church. Was discipline necessary for the very being of the church or was it simply about arrangements for good order? The second Book of Homilies is quite clear that there should be appropriate discipline in a biblically-ordered church and the Thirty-Nine Articles confirm this.

Whilst the church must endeavour everywhere and at all times to recognise how God is working in his world (for he has not left himself without witness anywhere – Acts 14:17), it must also be ever on guard against compromise with the spirit of the age. As we have seen, because of the origins of Anglicanism this can be a particular danger for Anglicans. The church is not primarily about expressing the religiosity or the values of a particular people at a particular time or place. If it is truly to be the church of Christ it will seek to bear witness to his good news, even when this goes against the spirit of the times. It will not shirk its prophetical role and will be committed to showing how God's unchanging word makes for authentic personal fulfilment and the common good.

The unity of the church is then a unity in diversity but 'how much' and 'what kind' of diversity is legitimate can only be identified by reference to the source of the unity as he is revealed in Scripture, which is the inspired and inspiring record of God's dealings with the whole of his creation. A unity in diversity which is properly both evangelical and catholic cannot simply be the result of negotiation, compromise and ambivalence. It must be soundly based on faithfulness to God's will as it is revealed in Scripture and in the church's constant witness to the apostolic teaching.

Successive Lambeth Conferences have told us that Anglicanism is not an end in itself. It is a means to an end as the church of God seeks to bear witness to the healing of the nations. In this sense, everything is provisional and if the historical forms of Anglicanism are lost for the sake of a more integral expression of the gospel and the greater unity of Christ's followers then that is something to be welcomed rather than feared. Those Anglicans who went into church union with Christians of other traditions were honouring this insight of the Lambeth Conferences. Alas, many other Anglicans did not follow them down this path. Whilst Anglicanism should be willing to lose itself in the cause of the gospel, it also bears particular gifts, ways of doing things and a theological and liturgical temperament which should not be neglected. It has, for example, expressed the common faith in a specific way from which others can profit. Its liturgical tradition has emphasised the importance of the vernacular in worship but also beauty and order. It is learning to balance spontaneity with a liturgical framework. It has seen that married clergy are in accordance with the teaching of Scripture and of the early church but it has also valued the call of celibacy for those whose ministry is enhanced in this way, by no means restricted to those in the religious communities. Whilst upholding the supremacy of Scripture, it has realised that this needs application in the numerous situations in which Christians find themselves. If we are to arrive at a proper estimate of the significance of Anglicanism for the future *both* its sense of identity and a willingness for provisionality will have to be taken into account.

In this Epilogue we have had, of necessity, to consider the more formal and institutional aspects of Anglicanism but if this book shows us anything it is the importance of people: mothers and thinkers like Susanna Wesley, political leaders like William Wilberforce and Lord Shaftesbury, preachers like Richard Sibbes, Charles Simeon and John Stott, and bishops like Thomas Cranmer and J.C. Ryle. It is not structures and formulae that are primary in the continuing mission of the church but people and the movements to which they give birth: the Wesleys and Methodism, the Clapham sect, the Church Mission Society and World Mission, the revival of religious communities and the establishing of theological colleges.

All of these have shaped the form of Anglicanism as we know it now. The structures and institutions have struggled to catch up. For today and tomorrow also, we need to look for those who are being raised up by God to teach, inspire, renew and equip his people. It is through people and God-given movements that a gospel-shaped future will be brought about. Our task is to be faithful, prayerful and open to God's work in our midst.

A truly mission-shaped church will not be shaped by human trends in fashion but by the Spirit of Christ constantly reminding it of what the Lord regards as essential, whatever the circumstances and culture in which it finds itself. Any change we embrace must ensure the effectiveness of the church's mission in bringing the eternal gospel to bear on the human need for healing and salvation. It must be biblically oriented and faithful to the apostolic preaching by which the church lives and which is also its missionary mandate. Nothing else and nothing less will do.

Notes

Thomas Cranmer

1. See R.T. Beckwith, 'The Prayer Book after Cranmer', in Cheslyn Jones, Geoffrey Wainwright, Edward Yarnold and Paul Bradshaw (eds), *The Study of Liturgy* (second edition, London, 1992); Marion J. Hatchett, 'Prayer Books', in Stephen Sykes, John Booty and Jonathan Knight (eds), *The Study of Anglicanism* (second edition, London, 1998); Charles Hefling and Cynthia Shattuck (eds), *The Oxford Guide to the Book of Common Prayer: A Worldwide Survey* (Oxford, 2006).
2. See especially, Diarmaid MacCulloch, *Tudor Church Militant: Edward VI and the Protestant Reformation* (London, 1999).
3. See Eamon Duffy, *The Stripping of the Altars: Traditional Religion in England c.1400-c.1580* (second edition, London, 2005); J.J. Scarisbrick, *Henry VIII* (London, 1968).
4. C.S. Carter, *The English Church and the Reformation* (London, 1912); A.G. Dickens, *The English Reformation* (second edition, London, 1989).
5. W.H. Frere, *A New History of the Book of Common Prayer*, with Francis Procter (revised edition, London, 1901); Gregory Dix, *The Shape of the Liturgy* (London, 1945).
6. Diarmaid MacCulloch, *Thomas Cranmer: A Life* (London, 1996), p. 1.
7. MacCulloch, *Cranmer*, p. 3.
8. The evidence is set out in H.I. Bailey, *The Liturgy Compared with the Bible* (London, 1833).
9. Article 6 of the Forty-Two Articles.
10. Dix, *Shape of the Liturgy*, p. 672.
11. Ashley Null, *Conversion to Communion: Thomas Cranmer on a Favourite Puritan Theme* (St Antholin's Lecture, London, 2000), p. 18.

Richard Hooker

1. John Keble (ed.), *The Works of that Learned and Judicious Divine Mr Richard Hooker* (3 vols, Oxford, 1836), vol. 1, p. civ.
2. See, for example, Peter Munz, *The Place of Hooker in the History of Thought* (London, 1952).
3. Hooker quoted in *A Christian Letter* (1599).
4. Richard Hooker, *Of the Lawes of Ecclesiastical Polity*, preface 1.2.
5. Hooker, *Lawes*, 1.4.1.
6. Hooker, *Lawes*, 1.8.9
7. Hooker, *Lawes*, 1.11.5.
8. Hooker, *Lawes*, 2.8.5.
9. Hooker, *Lawes*, 1.14.4.
10. Hooker, *Lawes*, 2.8.6.
11. Hooker, *Lawes*, preface 8.7.
12. Hooker, *Lawes*, 5.10.1.
13. Hooker, *Lawes*, 7.1.4.

Richard Sibbes

1. 'Yea and Amen', *The Works of Richard Sibbes* (7 vols, Edinburgh, 1973-83), vol. 4, p. 116.
2. 'Yea and Amen', *Works*, vol. 4, p. 116.
3. 'Yea and Amen', *Works*, vol. 4, p. 117.
4. 'The Soul's Conflict with Itself', *Works*, vol. 1, p. 250.
5. 'The Fountain Opened', *Works*, vol. 5, p. 469.
6. 'The Soul's Conflict with Itself', *Works*, vol. 1, p. 212.
7. 'The Soul's Conflict with Itself', *Works*, vol. 1, p. 215.
8. 'The Privileges of the Faithful', *Works*, vol. 5, p. 252.
9. 'The Fountain Opened', *Works*, vol. 5, p. 479.
10. 'The Rich Pearl', *Works*, vol. 7, p. 257.
11. 'Judgment's Reason', *Works*, vol. 4, p. 112.
12. 'The Power of Christ's Resurrection', *Works*, vol. 5, p. 198.
13. 'The Fountain Opened', *Works*, vol. 5, pp. 516-7.
14. 'Sibbes's Two Last Sermons; from Christ's Last Sermon', *Works*, vol. 7, p. 345.
15. 'The Excellency of the Gospel above the Law', *Works*, vol. 4, p. 215.
16. 'The Excellency of the Gospel above the Law', *Works*, vol. 4, p. 238.
17. 'The Excellency of the Gospel above the Law', *Works*, vol. 4, p. 239.
18. 'A Breathing after God', *Works*, vol. 2, p. 242.
19. 'The Fountain Opened', *Works*, vol. 5, p. 469.
20. 'The Fountain Opened', *Works*, vol.5, p. 507.
21. 'The Fountain Opened', *Works*, vol. 5, p. 504.
22. 'The Fountain Opened', *Works*, vol. 5, p. 509.

23. 'The Fountain Opened', *Works*, vol. 5, pp. 536-7.
24. 'The Privileges of the Faithful', *Works*, vol. 5, p. 277.
25. Written by Izaak Walton in his personal copy of Sibbes' *Returning Backslider* (1650).
26. 'A Consolatory Letter to an Afflicted Conscience', *Works*, vol. 1, p. cxvi.

Robert Boyle

1. For comments and corrections, I am most grateful to Professor Edward B. Davis, co-editor of the *The Works of Robert Boyle*.
2. Patrick Collinson, *The Religion of Protestants: The Church in English Society, 1559-1625* (Oxford, 1982), p. 90.
3. *Boyle by Himself and His Friends*, edited by Michael Hunter (London, 1994), p. 16.
4. Michael Hunter, 'Robert Boyle', *Oxford Dictionary of National Biography* (Oxford, 2004).
5. *Boyle by Himself and His Friends*, p. 48.
6. *Boyle by Himself and His Friends*, p. 104.
7. See Michael Hunter, *Robert Boyle (1627-1691): Scrupulosity and Conscience* (Woodbridge, 2000).
8. *The Correspondence of Robert Boyle*, edited by Michael Hunter, Antonio Clericuzio and Lawrence M. Principe (6 vols, London, 2001), vol. 1, pp. 33, 84, 68, 57, 133.
9. My account derives from Jan Wojcik, *Robert Boyle and the Limits of Reason* (Cambridge, 1997), Part I: 'The Theological Context'.
10. *The Works of Robert Boyle*, edited by Michael Hunter and Edward B. Davis (14 vols, London, 1999-2000), vol. 1, pp. 108-11. See also Wojcik, *Robert Boyle and the Limits of Reason*, ch. 3: 'Predestination Controversies'.
11. *Correspondence*, vol. 5, pp. 222-5.
12. The work diaries can be viewed online: http://www.livesandletters.ac.uk/wd/.
13. Cited in Denis Alexander, *Rebuilding the Matrix: Science and Faith in the Twenty-First Century* (Oxford, 2001), p. 140.
14. This point is developed in the introduction to Robert Boyle, *A Free Enquiry into the Vulgarly Received Notion of Nature*, edited by Edward B. Davis and Michael Hunter (Cambridge, 1996).
15. http://www.stmarylebow.co.uk/?Boyle_Lecture. See Alister McGrath, 'A Blast from the Past? The Boyle Lectures and Natural Theology', *Science and Christian Belief* 17 (2005), pp. 25-34.
16. http://www.bbk.ac.uk/boyle/.

Susanna Wesley

1. Maldwyn Edwards, *Family Circle* (London, 1949), p. 78.
2. John A. Newton, *Susanna Wesley and the Puritan Tradition in Methodism* (Peterborough, 2002), p. 108.
3. G. Elsie Harrison, *Son to Susanna* (London, 1937), pp. 25, 55, 323.
4. Charles Wallace, Jr, 'Wesley, Susanna', in *Oxford Dictionary of National Biography* (Oxford, 2004), vol. 58, p. 208.
5. Newton, *Susanna Wesley*, ch. 1; John A. Newton, 'Samuel Annesley (1620-1696)', *Proceedings of the Wesley Historical Society* 45 (1985), p. 33.
6. Charles Wallace, Jr, (ed.), *Susanna Wesley: The Complete Writings* (Oxford, 1997), pp. 5-7.
7. Richard P. Heitzenrater, *The Elusive Mr Wesley: John Wesley his own Biographer* (Nashville, 1984), vol. 1, pp. 38-43; Peter S. Forsaith, *John Wesley – Religious Hero?* (Oxford, 2004).
8. Wallace, *Complete Writings*, pp. 7, 93-9.
9. Newton, *Susanna Wesley*, p. 84.
10. Charles Wallace, Jr, 'Susanna Wesley's Spirituality: The Freedom of a Christian Woman', *Methodist History* 22 (1984), p. 161.
11. Newton, *Susanna Wesley*, p. 181; Henry D. Rack, *Reasonable Enthusiast: John Wesley and the Rise of Methodism* (London, 1989), p. 210.
12. Frank Baker, 'Susanna Wesley, Apologist for Methodism', *Proceedings of the Wesley Historical Society* 35 (1965), pp. 68-71.
13. Maurice Wiles, *Archetypal Heresy: Arianism through the Centuries* (Oxford, 1996), ch. 4, discusses the Trinitarian controversies of the late seventeenth century; Wallace, *Complete Writings*, pp. 356, 362
14. Wallace, *Complete Writings*, pp. 378, 380, 314-5.
15. Wallace, *Complete Writings*, pp. 308, 73, 149-50.
16. Wallace, *Complete Writings*, pp. 112-3; Herbert B. McGonigle, *John Wesley's Arminian Theology: An Introduction* (revised edition, Lutterworth, 2005), pp. 16-17. Compare Herbert B. McGonigle, *Sufficient Saving Grace: John Wesley's Evangelical Arminianism* (Carlisle, 2001), especially ch. 4.
17. Wallace, *Complete Writings*, pp. 149, 276.
18. Wallace, *Complete Writings*, pp. 108, 235, 234; compare Randy Maddox, *Responsible Grace: John Wesley's Practical Theology* (Nashville, 1994), ch. 3, especially pp. 81-2.
19. Wallace, *Complete Writings*, pp. 46-7.
20. Wallace, *Complete Writings*, p. 107.
21. Newton, *Susanna Wesley*, pp. 136-43.
22. Wallace, *Complete Writings*, p. 241.
23. Wallace, *Complete Writings*, pp. 272-3.
24. Newton, *Susanna Wesley*, pp. 32-6.
25. Wallace, *Complete Writings*, p. 276.
26. Wallace, *Complete Writings*, p. 73.
27. Newton, *Susanna Wesley*, pp. 197-8; W. Reginald Ward and Richard

P. Heitzenrater (eds), *The Works of John* Wesley, vol. 19, *Journal and Diaries II (1738-1743)* (Nashville, 1990), pp. 93-4.
28. Wallace, *Complete Writings*, p. 99.
29. Wallace, *Complete Writings*, p. 80.
30. Wallace, 'Susanna Wesley's Spirituality', p. 160.

William Wilberforce

1. William Wilberforce, *A Practical View of the Prevailing Religious System of Professed Christians in the Higher and Middle Classes in this Country, Contrasted with Real Christianity* (second edition, London, 1797), pp. 11-12.
2. Wilberforce, *Practical View*, p. 180.
3. Wilberforce, *Practical View*, pp. 117-8.
4. Wilberforce, *Practical View*, p. 12.
5. Wilberforce, *Practical View*, p. 84.
6. Wilberforce, *Practical View*, pp. 26-7.
7. Wilberforce, *Practical View*, pp. 121-2.
8. Wilberforce, *Practical View*, pp. 443-4.
9. Wilberforce, *Practical View*, pp. 136-7.
10. Wilberforce, *Practical View*, p. 64.
11. Wilberforce, *Practical View*, pp. 85-6.
12. Wilberforce, *Practical View*, pp. 87-9.
13. Wilberforce, *Practical View*, p. 84.
14. Wilberforce, *Practical View*, pp. 167-8.
15. Wilberforce, *Practical View*, p. 404.
16. Wilberforce, *Practical View*, p. 127.

Charles Simeon

1. G.O. Trevelyan, *The Life and Letters of Lord Macaulay* (2 vols, London, 1876), vol. 1, p. 68.
2. John King, *Memoir of the Rev. Thomas Dykes* (London, 1849), p. 8.
3. William Carus, *Memoirs of the Life of the Rev. Charles Simeon MA* (London, 1847), p. 9.
4. Charles Simeon, *Horae Homileticae, or Discourses, in the Form of Skeletons upon the Whole Scriptures* (21 vols, London, 1836), vol. 17, p. 339.
5. Simeon, *Horae Homileticae*, vol. 20, p. 188.
6. Simeon, *Horae Homileticae*, vol. 18, p. 502.
7. Simeon, *Horae Homileticae*, vol. 16, pp. 252-3.
8. Simeon, *Horae Homileticae*, vol. 11, p. 282.
9. Simeon, *Horae Homileticae*, vol. 1, p. xxvii.
10. Simeon, *Horae Homileticae*, vol. 16, p. 109.
11. A.W. Brown, *Recollections of the Conversation Parties of the Rev. Charles*

Simeon MA (London, 1863), pp. 61-2.

12. Simeon, *Horae Homileticae*, vol. 16, p. 56.
13. Simeon, *Horae Homileticae*, vol. 21, p. 281.
14. Simeon, *Horae Homileticae*, vol. 14, p. 581.
15. Simeon, *Horae Homileticae*, vol. 16, pp. 234-5.
16. Simeon, *Horae Homileticae*, vol. 15, p. 436.
17. Brown, *Recollections*, p. 267.
18. Simeon, *Horae Homileticae*, vol. 21, p. 281.
19. Simeon, *Horae Homileticae*, vol. 1, p. xiv.
20. Brown, *Recollections*, p. 132.
21. Brown, *Recollections*, p. 269.
22. Carus, *Memoirs*, p. 840.
23. Brown, *Recollections*, p. 58.
24. Brown, *Recollections*, pp. 11, 60.
25. Simeon, *Horae Homileticae*, vol. 16, p. 239.
26. Simeon, *Horae Homileticae*, vol. 6, p. 163; compare vol. 12, p. 437.
27. Simeon, *Horae Homileticae*, vol. 2, p. 246.
28. Simeon, *Horae Homileticae*, vol. 6, p. 162.
29. Simeon, *Horae Homileticae*, vol. 16, p. 245.
30. Simeon, *Horae Homileticae*, vol. 12, p. 436.
31. Simeon, *Horae Homileticae*, vol. 16, p. 407.
32. Simeon, *Horae Homileticae*, vol. 5, pp. 367-8.
33. Carus, *Memoirs*, pp. 844-5.
34. Charles Smyth, *Simeon and Church Order* (Cambridge, 1940), pp. 311, 255.
35. Smyth, *Simeon and Church Order*, p. 6.
36. K. Lake, *Memorials of William Charles Lake* (London, 1901), p. 52.
37. King, *Memoir of Thomas Dykes*, pp. 8-9.
38. Robert Pym, *Memoirs of the late Rev. William Nunn MA* (London, 1842), p. 72.
39. Francis Close, 'Reminiscences of the Rev. Charles Simeon', 16 October 1882, Simeon MSS, Ridley Hall, Cambridge.
40. Simeon, *Horae Homileticae*, vol. 1, p. xxi.
41. Simeon, *Horae Homileticae*, vol. 19, p. 90.
42. Brown, *Recollections*, p. 179.
43. Simeon, *Horae Homileticae*, vol. 1, p. xxii.
44. Thomas Hill (ed.) *Letters and Memoir of the late Walter Augustus Shirley DD* (London, 1849), p. 293.
45. H.C.G. Moule, *Charles Simeon* (London, 1892), p. 111.
46. H.E. Hopkins, *Charles Simeon of Cambridge* (London, 1977), p. 189.
47. W.T. Gidney, *The History of the London Society for Promoting Christianity amongst the Jews* (London, 1908), p. 273.
48. Brown, *Recollections*, p. 313.
49. Simeon, *Horae Homileticae*, vol. 15, p. 451.
50. Gidney, *History of LSPCJ*, p. 149.
51. Smyth, *Simeon and Church Order*, pp. xvi, 310.

52. Carus, *Memoirs*, p. 780.
53. Carus, *Memoirs*, pp. 747-8.
54. Carus, *Memoirs*, p. 748.
55. Carus, *Memoirs*, p. 749.
56. Francis Close, *A Brief Sketch of the Character and Last Days of the Rev. C. Simeon AM* (Cheltenham, 1836), pp. 17-8.

Lord Shaftesbury

1. He held the courtesy title of Lord Ashley from 1811, and became the seventh Earl of Shaftesbury in 1851. For simplicity, however, in this chapter he is throughout referred to as 'Shaftesbury'.
2. Lady Cowper and Lord Palmerston had a long-term adulterous relationship, and after Earl Cowper's death eventually married each other in 1839.
3. John Pollock, *Shaftesbury: The Poor Man's Earl* (London, 1985), pp. 19-21.
4. Edwin Hodder, *The Life and Work of the Seventh Earl of Shaftesbury, KG* (3 vols, London, 1886), vol. 1, pp. 43, 49. This original official biography remains useful, especially for the extensive, albeit carefully and sometimes misleadingly edited, extracts from the diaries. The original otherwise unpublished diaries are currently deposited in Southampton University Library.
5. Hodder, *Shaftesbury*, vol. 1, pp. 44, 53-6.
6. Hodder, *Shaftesbury*, vol. 1, pp. 87, 106, 110, 111.
7. Hodder, *Shaftesbury*, vol. 1, pp. 197-8.
8. Compare Geoffrey B.A.M. Finlayson, *The Seventh Earl of Shaftesbury 1801-1885* (London, 1982), pp. 49-52.
9. Hodder, *Shaftesbury*, vol. 2, pp. 284, 288; Finlayson, *Shaftesbury*, p. 505.
10. Hodder, *Shaftesbury*, vol. 2, p. 311.
11. The ellipsis contains the one observation on his friend which was inapplicable to Shaftesbury himself: Haldane's long life, he wrote, was one 'less of personal activity than of religious intellectualism'. The converse was obviously true of Shaftesbury, who although highly educated and intelligent, never had the time or inclination to be a systematic political or theological thinker.
12. Hodder, *Shaftesbury*, vol. 3, p. 449.
13. Finlayson, *Shaftesbury*, p. 320; Shaftesbury Papers, SHA/PD/3, 3 May 1845.
14. Hodder, *Shaftesbury*, vol. 1, pp. 147-9.
15. Quoted in Hodder, *Shaftesbury*, vol. 1, p. 455.
16. Hodder, *Shaftesbury*, vol. 1, p. 44
17. Hodder, *Shaftesbury*, vol. 1, p. 460.
18. Shaftesbury Papers, SHA/PD/4, 16 September 1846.
19. Finlayson, *Shaftesbury*, pp. 112, 252, 393, 581.
20. For a fuller account see John Wolffe, 'Lord Palmerston and Religion: A Reappraisal', *English Historical Review* 120 (2005), pp. 907-36.
21. Shaftesbury Papers, SHA/PD/1, 28 February 1829; Hodder, *Shaftesbury*, vol. 1, p. 174.

22. Edward Bickersteth, *Remarks on the Progress of Popery* (London, 1836), pp. 9-10; T.R. Birks, *Memoir of the Rev Edward Bickersteth* (second edition, 2 vols, London, 1852), vol. 2, p. 79.
23. Shaftesbury Papers, SHA/PD/5, 20 June, 17 November 1848.
24. Shaftesbury Papers, SHA/PD/5, 19 and 21 May 1849.
25. Shaftesbury Papers, SHA/PD/6, 20 March 1851; Finlayson, *Shaftesbury*, pp. 318, 320.
26. Shaftesbury Papers, SHA/PD/5, 8 April 1850.
27. Shaftesbury Papers, SHA/PD/6, 27 January 1851.
28. Hodder, *Shaftesbury*, vol. 3, p. 196.
29. Hodder, *Shaftesbury*, vol. 2, p. 334.
30. Finlayson, *Shaftesbury*, pp. 264-5; Hodder, *Shaftesbury*, vol. 3, p. 75.
31. I am indebted in this paragraph to Dr Donald Lewis for sight of the typescript of his forthcoming monograph on Shaftesbury and Christian Zionism. See also Finlayson, *Shaftesbury*, pp. 440-1, 582-3.
32. Hodder, *Shaftesbury*, vol. 1, p. 100.
33. Finlayson, *Shaftesbury*, pp. 207-8, 343-5, 447-60.
34. Pollock, *Shaftesbury*, p. 182.
35. Compare Finlayson, *Shaftesbury*, pp. 600-2.

J.C. Ryle

1. A condensed version of a paper given in Liverpool Cathedral on 2 July 2005 to mark the 125th anniversary of the foundation of the diocese. I am grateful to Liverpool Cathedral, Liverpool Hope University and the Historic Society of Lancashire and Cheshire for their invitation to speak, and to the Dean of Liverpool and Mrs Hoare for their hospitality.
2. *Liverpool Daily Post*, 11 May 1896, p. 5, quoted by Ian D. Farley, *J.C. Ryle, First Bishop of Liverpool: A Study in Mission amongst the Masses* (Carlisle, 2000), p. 121.
3. J.C. Ryle, *Is All Scripture Inspired? An Attempt to Answer the Question* (London, 1891), p. 73, quoted by Martin Wellings, *Evangelicals Embattled: Responses of Evangelicals in the Church of England to Ritualism, Darwinism and Theological Liberalism, 1890-1930* (Carlisle, 2003), p. 147.
4. Farley, *Ryle*, p. 36.
5. Peter Toon and Michael Smout, *John Charles Ryle, Evangelical Bishop* (Cambridge, 1976), p. 26.
6. Farley, *Ryle*, p. 120.
7. Farley, *Ryle*, p. 121.
8. J.C. Ryle, *Bishops and Clergy of Other Days: Or, the Lives of Two Reformers and Three Puritans* (London, 1868), p. 144.
9. Ryle, *Bishops and Clergy of Other Days*, p. 144.
10. J.C. Ryle, *Holiness* (London, 1879), p. xi.
11. J.C. Ryle, *Charges and Addresses* [1903] (Edinburgh, 1978), p. 95.

12. J.C. Ryle, *What is Wanted?* (1856), p. 38, quoted by Farley, *Ryle*, p. 73.

13. J.C. Ryle, *Be not Slothful but Followers* (1846), p. 38, quoted by Farley, *Ryle*, p. 31.

14. J.C. Ryle, *Tell Them* (1867), p. 11, quoted by Farley, *Ryle*, p. 31.

15. Ryle, *Charges and Addresses*, p. xii.

16. Ryle, *Charges and Addresses*, p. 63.

17. Ryle, *Charges and Addresses*, p. 295.

18. J.C. Ryle, *Church Reform* (London, 1870), p. 132.

19. Farley, *Ryle*, p. 116.

20. Farley, *Ryle*, p. 111.

21. Farley, *Ryle*, pp. 118-20, at p. 120 quoting *Liverpool Daily Post*, 1 February 1894, p. 3.

22. Farley, *Ryle*, pp. 90, 134, 99, 197.

23. Farley, *Ryle*, p. 95.

24. Farley, *Ryle*, p. 94.

25. Farley, *Ryle*, p. 112.

26. Ryle, *Church Reform*, p. 29.

27. Ryle, *Church Reform*, p. 31.

28. Farley, *Ryle*, p. 177.

29. Martin Wellings (ed.), 'J.C. Ryle: "First Words": An Opening Address delivered at the First Liverpool Diocesan Conference, 1881', in Mark Smith and Stephen Taylor (eds), *Evangelicalism in the Church of England, c.1790 – c.1890* (Woodbridge, 2004), pp. 296-9.

30. Toon and Smout, *Ryle*, p. 128.

31. Farley, *Ryle*, pp. 152-7.

32. *Albion*, 18 October 1880, quoted by Farley, *Ryle*, p. 146.

33. Farley, *Ryle*, p. 186; Ryle, *Charges and Addresses*, p. 294.

34. *Record*, 12 August 1892, p. 822, quoted by Wellings, *Evangelicals Embattled*, p. 111.

35. Farley, *Ryle*, pp. 158-9.

36. Ryle, *Bishops and Clergy*, p. xxi.

37. Farley, *Ryle*, pp. 92-3.

38. Ryle, *Charges and Addresses*, p. 19.

39. James Bentley, *Ritualism and Politics in Victorian Britain: The Attempt to Legislate for Belief* (Oxford, 1978), p. 115.

40. Farley, *Ryle*, p. 217.

41. Ryle, *Bishops and Clergy*, p. 123.

42. Farley, *Ryle*, p. 49; Toon and Smout, *Ryle*, p. 84.

43. Farley, *Ryle*, p. 49.

44. Farley, *Ryle*, p. 170.

45. *Church Congress Report* (1878), p. 388, quoted by Farley, *Ryle*, p. 52.

46. Farley, *Ryle*, p. 53.

47. Farley, *Ryle*, p. 90.

48. Ryle, *Charges and Addresses*, p. 28.

49. J.C. Ryle, *Knots Untied*, revised C.S. Carter (thirtieth edition, London, 1932), p. v.

Frances Ridley Havergal

1. Maria V.G. Havergal, *Memorials of Frances Ridley Havergal* (London, 1880), pp. 53-5.
2. Janet Grierson, *Frances Ridley Havergal: Worcestershire Hymnwriter* (Bromsgrove, 1979), p. 50.
3. Havergal, *Memorials*, p. 19.
4. Havergal, *Memorials*, pp. 233-4.
5. Havergal, *Memorials*, pp. 26-7.
6. Worcs. Record Office, Havergal's MS Autobiography, 27 Sept 1863, fo. 8.
7. MS Autobiography, 13 November 1864, fo. 16.
8. Havergal, *Memorials*, p. 73 (misleadingly conflated with the above passage).
9. MS Autobiography, 25 May 1867, fo. 29.
10. MS Autobiography, 27 September 1863, fo. 9.
11. Havergal, *Memorials*, pp. 125-7.
12. Havergal, *Memorials*, p. 135.
13. Havergal, *Memorials*, pp. 129, 131.
14. Grierson, *Havergal*, pp. 139-43.
15. Havergal, *Memorials*, p. 128.
16. Havergal, *Memorials*, p. 301.
17. Havergal, *Memorials*, p. 132.
18. Havergal, *Memorials*, pp. 204-5.
19. Grierson, *Havergal*, pp. 168-9.
20. Havergal, *Memorials*, pp. 234-5.
21. Havergal, *Memorials*, pp. 235-6.
22. Havergal, *Memorials*, p. 237.
23. Havergal, *Memorials*, pp. 177-8.
24. From the poems 'Is It For Me?' (1871) and 'My Master' (1876).
25. Havergal, *Memorials*, p. 187.
26. From the poem 'Another for Christ' (1872).
27. From the poem 'Glorified' (1871).
28. Havergal, *Memorials*, p. 267.
29. MS Autobiography, 7 May 1865, fo. 20.
30. Havergal, *Memorials*, p. 83.
31. Havergal, *Memorials*, p. 229.
32. From the poem 'What Thou Wilt' (1878).
33. Havergal, *Memorials*, p. 155, adapted from the poem 'The Moonlight Sonata' (1869).
34. Havergal, *Memorials*, p. 20.
35. Havergal, *Memorials*, pp. 223-4.
36. Havergal, *Memorials*, p. 62.
37. Havergal, *Memorials*, p. 157.
38. Havergal, *Memorials*, p. 186.
39. Havergal, *Memorials*, p. 221.
40. Havergal, *Memorials*, p. 290.
41. Havergal, *Memorials*, pp. 303-6.

C.S. Lewis

1. John Wain, 'A Great Clerke' in James T. Como (ed.), *Remembering C.S. Lewis: Recollections of Those Who Knew Him* (San Francisco, 2005), p. 155.
2. C.S. Lewis, *Surprised by Joy: The Shape of My Early Life* (Glasgow, 1982), pp. 189-90.
3. C.S. Lewis, *Mere Christianity* (Glasgow, 1990), p. 8.
4. C.S. Lewis, *The Problem of Pain* (Glasgow, 1983), p. viii.
5. C.S. Lewis, *The Pilgrim's Regress: An Allegorical Apology for Christianity, Reason and Romanticism* (Glasgow, 1980), p. 21.
6. C.S. Lewis, *English Literature in the Sixteenth Century, Excluding Drama* (Oxford, 1954), p. 33.
7. E.M.W. Tillyard and C.S. Lewis, *The Personal Heresy, A Controversy* (London, 1965), p. 11.
8. Lewis, *Surprised by Joy*, p. 59.
9. Lewis, *Surprised by Joy*, p. 139.
10. Lewis, *Surprised by Joy*, p. 155.
11. Lewis, *Surprised by Joy*, p. 181.
12. Lewis, *Surprised by Joy*, pp. 36, 98-103.
13. Lewis, *Surprised by Joy*, p. 130.
14. Joy Davidman, *Smoke on the Mountain: An Interpretation of the Ten Commandments in terms of to-day* (London, 1955), p. 7.
15. Lewis, *Mere Christianity*, p. 109.
16. Owen Barfield, 'Introduction to *Light on C.S. Lewis*' in Owen Barfield, *Owen Barfield on C.S. Lewis*, edited by G.B. Tennyson (Middletown, CT, 1989), pp. 24-5.
17. Lewis, *Mere Christianity*, p. 125.
18. Lewis, *Mere Christianity*, p. 126.
19. C.S. Lewis, *The Voyage of the 'Dawn Treader'* (Glasgow, 1981), p. 86.
20. Lewis, *The Pilgrim's Regress*, p. 216.
21. C.S. Lewis, *The Four Loves* (Glasgow, 1991), p. 120.
22. Lewis, *The Voyage of the 'Dawn Treader'*, p. 52.
23. Lewis, *Surprised by Joy*, p. 174.
24. 'Meditation in a Toolshed', in C.S. Lewis, *Essay Collection*, edited by Lesley Walmsley (London, 2000), p. 607.
25. Lewis, *Surprised by Joy*, p. 175.
26. Lewis, *Mere Christianity*, p. 149.
27. C.S. Lewis, *Prayer: Letters to Malcolm* (London, 1983), p. 23.
28. Lewis, *Mere Christianity*, p. 129.
29. Lewis, *Letters to Malcolm*, p. 71.
30. Lewis, *Letters to Malcolm*, p. 77.
31. Letter to Mary Willis Shelburne, 20 February 1955, in C.S. Lewis, *Collected Letters*, edited by Walter Hooper (3 vols, London, 2000-6), vol. 3, p. 567.
32. C.S. Lewis, *George MacDonald: An Anthology* (San Francisco, 2001), p. 102.

33. C.S. Lewis, *Reflections on the Psalms* (Glasgow, 1984), p. 95.
34. See Lewis, *Mere Christianity*, pp. 53-8; letter to Mr Young, 31 October 1963, in Lewis, *Collected Letters*, vol. 3, p. 1476.
35. Lewis, *Reflections on the Psalms*, p. 94.
36. Lewis, *Letters to Malcolm*, p. 106.
37. Lewis, *Surprised by Joy*, p. 189.
38. 'Cross-Examination', in Lewis, *Essay Collection*, p. 553.
39. Lewis, *Surprised by Joy*, p. 20.
40. Lewis, *Surprised by Joy*.
41. Lewis, *Surprised by Joy*, p. 12.
42. Lewis, *Surprised by Joy*, pp. 18-9.
43. 'The Weight of Glory', in Lewis, *Essay Collection*, p. 98.
44. To Stephen Medcalf goes the distinction of having noticed this artistic licence. Lewis recalls how there were bluebells underfoot in Wallaby Wood when he arrived at Whipsnade Zoo. The only problem is that he made the journey in September when bluebells are not in flower. Perhaps he genuinely misremembered and confused the visit with another he made a few months later. More probably, as a poet and 'votary of the Blue Flower', he decided to set the experience in spring-time in order artistically to suggest the spring-time of his soul. See Stephen Medcalf, 'Language and Self-Consciousness: The Making and Breaking of C.S. Lewis's Personae' in Peter J. Schakel and Charles A. Huttar (eds), *Word and Story in C.S. Lewis* (Columbia, 1991), pp. 109-44.
45. Lewis, *Mere Christianity*, pp. 188-9.

John Stott

1. Timothy Dudley-Smith, *John Stott: The Making of a Leader* (Leicester, 1999), pp. 254-5.
2. Oliver Barclay, *Evangelicalism in Britain 1935-1995* (Leicester, 1997), p. 84. See also David F. Wells, 'Evangelical: Some Theological Differences and Similarities' in Mark Noll, David Bebbington and George Rawlyk (eds), *Evangelicalism: Comparative Studies of Popular Protestantism in North America, the British Isles, and Beyond 1700-1990* (Oxford, 1994), pp. 393-8.
3. John Stott, *Evangelical Truth: A Personal Plea for Unity, Integrity and Faithfulness* (Downers Grove, 1999), p. 25.
4. David L. Edwards with John Stott, *Evangelical Essentials: A Liberal-Evangelical Dialogue* (Downers Grove, 1988), p. 84. See also Roger Steer, *Guarding the Holy Fire: The Evangelicalism of John Stott, J.I. Packer, and Alister McGrath* (Grand Rapids, 1999), p. 239.
5. John Stott, 'The Anglican Communion and Scripture', in *Anglican Communion and Scripture: Papers from the First International Consultation of the Evangelical Fellowship in the Anglican Communion, Canterbury, UK, June 1993* (Oxford, 1996), p. 13.

6. John Stott, *Christ the Controversialist: A Study of Essentials of Evangelical Religion* (Downers Grove, 1974), pp. 49-64.

7. Edwards with Stott, *Evangelical Essentials*, pp. 219-33.

8. John Stott, *I Believe in Preaching* (London, 1982), pp. 94-5.

9. Stott, 'The Anglican Communion and Scripture', p. 25.

10. B.B. Warfield, *The Inspiration and Authority of the Bible* (Philadelphia, 1948), pp. 299-347.

11. David Samuel (ed.), *The Evangelical Succession in the Church of England* (Cambridge, 1979), p. 5.

12. This was the reformers' belief summed up as the 'analogy of faith' which Stott endorsed. See Stott, *I Believe in Preaching*, p. 128.

13. The quotation is from the Lausanne Covenant which Stott drafted for the International Congress on World Evangelization in 1974. For commentary on the phrase 'in all that it affirms', see Stott's *The Lausanne Covenant: An Exposition and Commentary* (Wheaton, 1975), p. 7. However, as he told Edwards, 'I confess that I have never myself been greatly enamoured of the word "inerrancy" mainly because I prefer a single positive ("true" or "trustworthy") to a double negative ("inerrant", or for that matter "infallible", which is its British equivalent).'; Edwards with Stott, *Evangelical Essentials*, p. 95. If Stott did not favour the language of inerrancy, he nevertheless retained the idea it was seeking to protect.

14. Edwards with Stott, *Evangelical Essentials*, p. 85. This is a consistently worked out theme. For example, after reviewing Paul's autobiography in Galatians 2:11-24, Stott observes that if 'Paul was right in asserting that his gospel was not man's but God's (cf. Rom. 1:1), then to reject Paul is to reject God'; John Stott, *The Message of Galatians* (Leicester, 1968), p. 37.

15. J.I. Packer, 'Authority in Preaching', in Martyn Eden and David F. Wells (eds), *The Gospel in the Modern World: A Tribute to John Stott* (Downers Grove, 1991), p. 198.

16. John Stott, *Between Two Worlds: The Art of Preaching in the Twentieth Century* (Grand Rapids, 1982), pp. 92-134.

17. Philip Edgcumbe Hughes, *Theology of the English Reformers* (London, 1965), pp. 121-7.

18. Stott, *I Believe in Preaching*, p. 115.

19. John Stott, *The Preacher's Portrait* (London, 1967), p. 20.

20. Stott, *I Believe in Preaching*, p. 126.

21. Stott, *I Believe in Preaching*, p. 37.

22. See, for example, John Stott and Robert Coote (eds), *Down to Earth: Studies in Christianity and Culture* (Wheaton, 1980).

23. John Stott, *Decisive Issues Facing Christians Today* (Grand Rapids, 1984).

24. Stott said that God the Father is the author of biblical revelation, the Holy Spirit its agent, and Christ is 'both the principal subject and authenticating witness.' John Stott, *God's Book for God's People* (Downers Grove, 1982), p. 61.

25. Stott, *Message of Galatians*, p. 80.

26. Stott, *Message of Galatians*, p. 89.
27. John Stott, *The Cross of Christ* (Nottingham, 1986), p. 125.
28. Stott, *Cross of Christ*, p. 145.
29. Stott, *Cross of Christ*, p. 175.
30. Stott, *Cross of Christ*, pp. 166-8. In this act, Stott insisted that our sin is not simply expiated but God's wrath is also propitiated. See his comments on 1 John 2:2 and 4:10 and especially the extended note in *The Epistles of John: An Introduction and Commentary* (London, 1964), pp. 84-8.
31. Stott, *Evangelical Truth*, p. 107.
32. Stott, *Message of Galatians*, p. 34.
33. John Stott, *Baptism and Fullness: The Work of the Holy Spirit Today* (Downers Grove, 1964), p. 39.
34. John Stott, *Your Confirmation* (London, 1958), p. 19; John Stott, 'But the Bible Says . . . About Baptism and Salvation', *Crusade* 13 (December 1967), pp. 40-1.
35. See John Stott, 'A Note About the Stuttgart Statement on Evangelism', in Vinay Samuel and Albrecht Hauser (eds), *Proclaiming Christ in Christ's Way* (Oxford, 1989), pp. 208-11.
36. See Arthur P. Johnston, *The Battle for World Evangelism* (Wheaton, 1978) pp. 291-306.
37. See John Stott (ed.), *Making Christ Known: Historic Mission Documents from the Lausanne Movement, 1974-1989* (Grand Rapids, 1996), pp. 165-210.

David Watson

1. David Watson, *You Are My God: An Autobiography* (London, 1983), pp. 184-7.
2. David Watson, *I Believe in the Church* (London, 1978), p. 13.
3. David Watson, *Study Guide: I Believe in the Church* (London, 1982), p. 10.
4. Teddy Saunders and Hugh Sansom, *David Watson: A Biography* (London, 1992), p. 186.
5. Saunders and Sansom, *David Watson*, p. 156.
6. David Watson, *Discipleship* (London, 1981), p. 147.
7. Watson, *You Are My God*, pp. 51-3.
8. David Watson, *One in the Spirit* (London, 1973), p. 13.
9. Watson, *One in the Spirit*, p. 70.
10. David Watson, *I Believe in Evangelism* (London, 1976), p. 171.
11. Watson, *Discipleship*, p. 194.
12. Saunders and Sansom, *David Watson*, pp. 22-3.
13. Saunders and Sansom, *David Watson*, p. 175.
14. Saunders and Sansom, *David Watson*, p. 84.
15. Watson, *One in the Spirit*, p. 74.
16. David Watson, *Fear No Evil: A Personal Struggle with Cancer* (London, 1984), p. 109.

17. Watson, *You Are My God*, p. 63.
18. Watson, *One in the Spirit*, p. 81.
19. Watson, *One in the Spirit*, p. 44.
20. Gordon D. Fee, *God's Empowering Presence: The Holy Spirit in the Letters of Paul* (Peabody, Massachusetts, 1994).
21. Watson, *I Believe in the Church*, p. 179.
22. Watson, *I Believe in the Church*, pp. 197-8.
23. Watson, *I Believe in Evangelism*, p. 156.
24. Watson, *I Believe in Evangelism*, p. 136.
25. See, for example, *One in the Spirit*, ch. 3; *I Believe in the Church*, ch. 7; *Discipleship*, chs 2-3.
26. Watson, *I Believe in the Church*, p. 110.
27. Watson, *I Believe in the Church*, chs 15-16. When Watson wrote these chapters, his thinking about the role of women in leadership was still in transition. He settled eventually on the view that all of the leadership roles in the church were open to all, on the basis of gift and calling, irrespective of gender.
28. Watson, *Discipleship*, p. 50.
29. Watson, *Discipleship*, p. 56.
30. Watson, *Discipleship*, p. 60.
31. Watson, *I Believe in the Church*, p. 174.
32. See Watson, *Discipleship*, ch. 10 and Appendix A. Watson wrote the foreword to the British edition of Ronald J. Sider, *Rich Christians in an Age of Hunger: A Biblical Study* (London, 1978).
33. See David Watson, 'Simple Lifestyle and Evangelism', in Ronald J. Sider (ed.), *Lifestyle in the Eighties: An Evangelical Commitment to Simple Lifestyle* (Exeter, 1982).
34. Saunders and Sansom, *David Watson*, p. 192.
35. Saunders and Sansom, *David Watson*, p. 186.
36. Watson, *Discipleship*, p. 51.
37. Personal recollection from a sermon at St Michael-le-Belfrey 'Renewal Week'.
38. Watson, *Discipleship*, pp. 243-4.
39. Watson, *Fear No Evil*, p. 107.
40. Watson, *Fear No Evil*, p. 168.
41. Watson, *Fear No Evil*, p. 146.
42. Watson, *Fear No Evil*, p. 164.
43. Watson, *Fear No Evil*, p. 172.
44. Watson, *Fear No Evil*, pp. 168, 172
45. Edward England (ed.), *David Watson: A Portrait By His Friends* (Crowborough, 1985), p. 210.

Further Reading

Atkinson, Nigel, *Richard Hooker and the Authority of Scripture, Tradition and Reason* (second edition, Vancouver, 2005)

Best, G.F.A., *Shaftesbury* (London, 1964)

Bray, Gerald, *Documents of the English Reformation* (new edition, Cambridge, 2006)

Brooks, Peter Newman, *Cranmer in Context* (Cambridge, 1989)

Brooks, Peter Newman, *Thomas Cranmer's Doctrine of the Eucharist* (second edition, Basingstoke, 1992)

Brydon, Michael, *The Evolving Reputation of Richard Hooker: An Examination of Responses, 1600-1714* (Oxford, 2006)

Como, James T. (ed.), *Remembering C.S. Lewis: Recollections of Those Who Knew Him* (San Francisco, 2005)

Davis, Edward B., 'Robert Boyle's Religious Life, Attitudes and Vocation', *Science and Christian Belief* 19 (2007), pp. 117-38

Dever, Mark, *Richard Sibbes: Puritanism and Calvinism in Late Elizabethan and Early Stuart England* (Macon, Georgia, 2000)

Dudley-Smith, Timothy, *John Stott: A Global Ministry* (Leicester, 2001)

Dudley-Smith, Timothy, *John Stott: The Making of a Leader* (Leicester, 1999)

Evans, G.R., *John Wyclif: Myth and Reality* (Oxford, 2005)

Evans, G.R., *The Church in the Early Middle Ages* (London, 2007)

Farley, Ian D., *J.C. Ryle, First Bishop of Liverpool: A Study in Mission amongst the Masses* (Carlisle, 2000)

Finlayson, Geoffrey B.A.M., *The Seventh Earl of Shaftesbury 1801-1885* (London, 1982)

Green, Roger Lancelyn, and Walter Hooper, *C.S. Lewis: A Biography* (revised and expanded edition, London, 2002)

Grierson, Janet, *Frances Ridley Havergal: Worcestershire Hymnwriter* (Bromsgrove, 1979)

Havergal, Maria V.G., *Memorials of Frances Ridley Havergal* (London, 1880)

Hopkins, Hugh Evan, *Charles Simeon of Cambridge* (London, 1977)

Hunter, Michael (ed.), *Robert Boyle by Himself and His Friends* (London, 1994)

Hunter, Michael (ed.), *Robert Boyle: Scrupulosity and Conscience* (Woodbridge, 2000)

Kirby, Torrance W.J., *Richard Hooker: Reformer and Platonist* (Aldershot, 2005)

MacCulloch, Diarmaid, *Thomas Cranmer: A Life* (London, 1996)

Moule, Handley, *Charles Simeon* (new edition, Fearn, Ross-shire, 1997)

Newton, John A., *Susanna Wesley and the Puritan Tradition in Methodism* (revised edition, Peterborough, 2002).

Null, Ashley, *Thomas Cranmer's Doctrine of Repentance* (Oxford, 2001)

Pollock, John, *Shaftesbury: The Poor Man's Earl* (London, 1985)

Pollock, John, *Wilberforce* (new edition, Eastbourne, 2007)

Saunders, Teddy, and Hugh Sansom, *David Watson: A Biography* (London, 1992)

Toon, Peter, and Michael Smout, *John Charles Ryle, Evangelical Bishop* (Cambridge, 1976)

Wallace, Charles (ed.), *Susanna Wesley: The Complete Writings* (Oxford, 1997)

Ward, Benedicta, *The Venerable Bede* (new edition, London, 2002)

Ward, Michael, *Planet Narnia: The Seven Heavens in the Imagination of C.S. Lewis* (New York, 2008)

Watson, David, *You Are My God: An Autobiography* (London, 1983)

Watson, David, *Fear No Evil: A Personal Struggle with Cancer* (London, 1984)

Wojcik, Jan, *Robert Boyle and the Limits of Reason* (Cambridge, 1997)

Wolffe, John, *The Expansion of Evangelicalism: The Age of Wilberforce, More, Chalmers and Finney* (Nottingham, 2006)

Index of Names

Printed in the United Kingdom
by Lightning Source UK Ltd.
131281UK00001B/25-36/P